Sabbaths, Sacraments, and Seasons

by Arnold Kenseth

A Collection of Meditations, Prayers, and Canticles

Pilgrim Press Philadelphia Boston

Illustrated by Joachim Pfeufer

Library of Congress Catalog Card Number 71-96298

The publisher wishes to express appreciation to the *United Church Herald* for permission to reprint the material on pages 11–17, 67 (1st prayer), 89 (2d prayer), 96, 101 (1st and 2d prayers), 102, 103 (3d prayer) from December 1968 issue (Vol. XI, No. 12).

To my mother and father
for life and love

Acknowledgment

I acknowledge gratefully the imaginative people of South Congregational Church in Amherst who permitted the use of these devotions as a regular part of morning worship. I thank many friends close by and at a distance who urged that such a book as this might encourage the praise of God and the love of man and, in particular, I thank Miriam Richards, Barbara Dodge, and Madeline de Friesse, who put the manuscript in good order and kept my spirits high.

Sabbaths, Sacraments, and Seasons

Sabbaths

December — First Sunday

We know inside ourselves our own darknesses; or, if we do not know them or understand them, we feel them brooding in us as sadness and silences, startling lusts, fears whispering, echoing chasms where we seem to stand at the brink of all man's grief. And the winter that invariably comes surrounds us visibly with the cold and the dark and the death that invisibly we live with every day and in all seasons. And at this time of our despair the cry of Advent reverberates across our lives. "Watchman, tell us of the night, what are its signs of promise?" The answer that comes is not given by man for such an answer would only be darkness speaking to darkness. Rather there comes a transcendent Word, an eternal shout of joy, a promise signed in heaven itself. There comes the word of divine comfort. In our sophistications we may not hear it, we may turn from it, we may despise it. If so, our dark remains dark, and we continue to be of all men the most miserable and the most foolish.

December — First Sunday

O Lord, the watchmen of ten thousand times ten thousand cities cry to the winter night the news of thy coming. Even so, we praise thee, Word of Light to our darkness, Word of Peace to our warfare, Word of Love to our fear. Let carols sing, let prayers adore, let the whole earth rejoice and declare thee. Thou art fire and garland. Thou art the good shepherd and the true king. With angels and archangels we adore thee, world without end. Amen.

O God, we are strangers and sojourners, except thou art with us. We are no people, except we are thy people. Our very days are lost, except we find them in thee. We know no mercy, except we receive thy mercy. Come to us. Sing in us new songs. Teach our prayers our needs. Give us thyself. Be our defender against the evil day and the false prosperity. And set our feet on the paths that run toward Bethlehem. Amen.

We are making ready, Lord. Our hearts are hillsides listening. Our minds are hastening footsteps. Our bodies are a cradle. Our whole being is praise and rejoicing. And unto thee be the glory, O Word made flesh, in whose peace we are secure, in whose mercy we are forgiven, and in whose love we are redeemed, forever and ever. Amen.

December — Second Sunday

There can be no doubt that at heart and in the very marrow of all that life and death means, the news of the birth of the Savior comes as tidings of comfort and joy. Thus, the old carol is right when it declares, "God rest ye merry gentlemen, let nothing you dismay." We are properly merry. We are to be at peace within ourselves. We are not to fear. But these things are only true for us when we rejoice in God, when we live in his peace, when we trust in his strength. Nevertheless there is irony in our making such observations, since we live in an age and are people of a generation that does not understand them. For if we perceive the meaning of the peace of God, we instinctively know that when it comes to us, it endangers us. When God comes—and he is always coming—the proud are scattered, the mighty are put down, the rich are sent empty away. These are the words of the Magnificat. They precede the Birth. They are words of warning sung within a song of exceeding great joy.

December — Second Sunday

Clamorous, O Lord, is this season of thy birth, this snowfall air with heaven's love in it, this darkened time ablaze with more than light, this age of warfares suddenly abound with peace, these days abrim with innocence, this century upon its knees, this good eternity. O blessed One, give us thy joy and let us arise to know thy mornings in our nights. Amen.

Blessed Lord, in this season of thy coming, the darkness in us deepens awaiting thy Light, the evil in us trembles expecting thy Mercy, the knowledge in us falters hearing thy Truth. O we have sinned against innocence, forgotten human sorrow, denied pity, excused ourselves from love, and shunned holiness. Assail us by the bright blows of thy grace and make us teachable, that we may learn again the peace that comes on earth to men of goodwill; through Jesus Christ our Lord. Amen.

O that our tongues were bells and our hands drums and our feet a dance and a leap that we might praise thee. Could the winter day but say for us our praise or the brittle grass or the air on the blue jay's wing. Where is the music that shall sing thee? What word shall tell the heart's adoration? O Majesty, let us but kneel in the mind's dark, in the body's rush, in the soul's aloneness, and hear thee being born. Amen.

December — Third Sunday

It is the time of our remembering again the coming of the One who saves. The winter is about us, the season whose signature is wide: clear in the daytime and in the night the ever-descending, ever longer dark. It is the season long in the memory of man for speaking the ancient signs of the year's ending and man's ending. "The woods are lovely, dark and deep"; the air frosts as we breathe; the ground is hard. We listen to our souls upon the wind. We lean to the motion of the stars and wait as children for the distant music to begin again. For at this climax of another year, of closing in, of dying, of death, we hear another word of beginning and of birth. And we remember the One who comes and abides—a bearer of lightning that banishes darkness, a healer of sicknesses, a reconciler of warfares, a giver of forgiveness. His name shall be called "Emmanuel," which being translated means "God with us."

December — Third Sunday

We thank thee, O Heaven, O Highest, O most Blessed. We praise thee, O Brightness beyond us yet by us, surrounding, invading, within and without us! We glorify thee, O Mystery, O Mercy, O most Holy. We adore thee, O Word shaped in love, spoken in fire, captured in flesh, and given for our sins. We thank, we praise, we glorify, we adore thee, Father, Son, and Holy Ghost. Amen.

Dear Lord, what is it in us dreads thy coming? Why do the palms of our hands cover our eyes lest our souls see thee? When the music sounds from the far heaven, we tremble, and when it sounds like bells and truth close by us, our very hearts cry out a gladness long forgotten yet always long remembered. It is our sin that dreads and hides. Our pride cannot bear thee. Our falsehood cannot hear thee. O gracious One, come even so and devastate us and empty us, and, in thy mercy, capture us for joy. Amen.

O God, for whatever in us reaches for thy coming, we rejoice in thy name. Praise for the fir tree and the candled dark. Praise for the hush and the crunch on snow. Praise for the hiddenness and hope and bold surprise. Praise for the shepherd's crook, three kings, and Mary bowed. Praise for bells and chiming balls tossed in the high night. Praise for God's good Son, thy sparrow in our barn, thy Word within our flesh, thy alleluia in our hearts. Amen. Amen. Amen.

Christmas Day

Christmas is happening again in our strange human hearts—strange, because into a season of holiness we have let intrude the idols of our human vanity and greed, but hearts, nonetheless, that desire to love and to honor God. At the level of our love for God we are pressed into a celebration to which the most lively wonder of our being responds. We are aware of the hidden depths in things and people. We have a sense of going beneath the surfaces to surpluses of strength and beauty we had forgotten were there. We have, perhaps unconsciously, a felt amazement at belonging to a history that goes back to the beginning of time. We dwell again in the mystery of God. Moreover, we see people differently. For a little while there returns in us every impulse of tenderness toward even our enemies. We hear with new sadness the cry of the sick, the lonely, and the condemned. The anguish of our wars is exposed in us bitterly. But, even more, we reach out our hands to heal; we would with Isaiah give to all men "the oil of joy for mourning, the garment of praise for the spirit of heaviness." We live within the compassion of God, and we perceive that to live well is to live simply. We are recaptured by the small and the innocent and the chaste. To the work of our hands is added the glory of God; to the food on our table and the family that eats it, is given the blessing of God. Everything is true within the praise we sing: "O come, let us adore him." For when we adore him, we have found our meaning. We are becoming the children of God.

Christmas Day

O Lord, in this alien time, this out-of-season century, this age absurd and wonderful and lost, we cry thy name whose name we cannot cry. O thou who art always coming, come! And give our voices praise and our eyes thy mystery. Let us taste thee in all our winter loneliness and let us hear thee as a shout against our long despair—till touched by grace, our griefs become our joys. Teach us to run with shepherds and to kneel with kings. Amen.

O God, we, thy sometime people, avoid thee as we can, because thy storming grace cuts us down to size and thy love devastates us. We have cushioned ourselves against our mortality. We have turned away from the times and places where the holy mysteries take our true measure. We want thy magic but not thy judgment. O make us ashamed that we can settle for the crumbs that are our plenty, and show us in the clear glass of thy coming among us how peace must speak to wars, mercy to brokenness, and love to fear. Let the blazing birth burn us down to honesty about our need of thy hand upon us, thy joy within our hearts. Amen.

O God, what curious praise is ours for Jesus Christ: a red tricycle for small and busy feet, skis for a boy to ride the wind, some perfumes for the body's love, a large check for sweet charity, two hundred Christmas cards signed "love" by hand, letters to friends long lost in years ago, much weariness and ribbons and short tempers. O find in this, O find in this, dear Lord, our human hearts, our hope for men, our praise for thee! For we stumble in the busy ways and have a lonely carol to sing before the holy places. In Jesus' name. Amen.

What is, perhaps, most disturbing is the time after the celebration. The festivity, the days of Christmas, sang over us and in us, and we found voices of rejoicing that we did not remember but which had always been there. All around us we saw the bright against the dark, the good conquering the evil, hope overtaking despair—and all this taking place with flourish and gaiety and great gladness. The return to the normal, the motion back from the blaze to the gray, the walk on streets that no longer fill with chiming bells—this is our human necessity. We cannot bear God in all his clamorous glory for long. And yet it is for people like us in this average, day-to-day, hour-by-hour routine that Christ was born. If this were not so, the huge grace of Christmas would be a fraud. For it is to hearten us in the boredom, to awaken us in the drowsy plodding, to make us whole and lively among the broken pieces of life—it is for these things that God came among us. True, we can escape into the little meager purposes we make to keep us busy, to keep us from the daring of God's purposes in our midst. But, as is told in the Gospels, Jesus stops at every doorstep, waits at every ordinary door.

December

Fourth Sunday

At the year's end, vast God, our hearts praise thee. Yea, for our sakes thy wisdom becomes foolishness, thy power weakness, thy heaven a manger, thyself a Child. So are our bodies full of thy song, our minds brimming with thy peace, and our souls merry with thy joy. Blessed be thy name forever and ever. Amen.

Almighty and gracious, high and holy God, we blunder through the days of our lives in vague and harried disorder, seeking the pleasures that give us no Joy, seeking the securities that give us no Peace, seeking the knowledge that gives us no Truth, seeking the community that gives us no Love. O Lord, turn us again to seek the city which hath foundations, and stand us in the places of thy holy fire where facade and falsehood burn away and where thy grace fashions us again into lively and exultant souls. Amen.

We pray that this day we shall give thee true praise, O great Lord. May our worship be honest and tell thee our true needs and speak our gladness in the gifts given by thy mercy: life in the bones, a winterfall of air against the cheeks, suppertime with love, forgiveness when all seemed lost, a march of children, books on the shelves, sleep's reassurance, and thyself in the midst of it all. O make us thine own always. Amen.

January — First Sunday

How marvelously the year's end has become for contemporary man a gathering-up of all his triumphs and defeats, a weighing in the balance of human experience, shining and dark, that has happened in the last twelvemonth. There is a searching backward for the events of size, excitement, achievement as mankind tries with almost teen-age zeal to total up the score. What did the human race do last year? And, having asked that question, for some people there arises the question: What does it all mean? The ritual is an old one and a good one; and from it we press on to the new year and the new hope. And, as in more ancient days, men, looking into the mysteries that lie ahead, still prophesy and dream dreams. It is in the context of the very mystery of all human events that the Christian man stands with an advantage. For at the very closing down of the year and at the very edge of the new year, he has celebrated both the meaning of the year gone by and the hope of the year that lies ahead. He has seen "the glory of the Lord revealed" and known in his heart the Light by whose penetration time past, time present, and time future are given "the garland of joy instead of the ashes of mourning."

January — First Sunday

O timeless Lord of all our days and years, now as the twelve months close and we remember and reflect: provide us with thyself as companion as we enter the new year. Put from us, in the mercy of thy means, the waste of hours, the dry seasons, the desolate evenings, and the shabby dawns. Go with us into the mystery of the days that run in haste before us. Show us the everlasting in the perishable, the hope in the defeat, the purpose in the chaos. Help us arise to each morning, glad that its seconds have the height of thine eternity; through Jesus Christ our Lord. Amen.

O God, our days go by as a dream and the seasons run swiftly on and are gone; and we do not turn to thee, nor hear thy Word, nor look for thee in the night watches. We walk in the mazes of our own vanity. We listen to the prattle of foolish men. And in the dark of our own dark, we look into our own blind eyes. O holy, high, and mighty Lord, break us loose from our folly. Capture us by grace and hold us in mercy, lest our years go by empty, drab, and lost. Save us through Jesus Christ our Lord. Amen.

O God, we praise thee for thyself in whom we live and by whom all things are sanctified and made for shining. We praise thee for this day which proceeds from thy bounty and returns to thy love. We praise thee for every moment when the work of our hands is blessed beyond our deserving and for every hour that our hearts are made glad by a wise and endless peace we did not earn. Amen.

January *Second Sunday*

"Thou shalt love the Lord thy God with all thy heart . . ."

There is the love of the heart toward God. When it happens in a man, it is a warm uncalculating affair not unlike falling in love for the first time. It makes an ordinary man into a St. Francis; and when it occurs among a whole people, most extraordinary things follow among neighbors and between enemies. The love of God that the heart knows is very tangible. Just as the lover must somehow shower the beloved with gifts and acts of graciousness, so those who love God with the heart set about finding ways to please him. There is no special place we begin, no order in which this love is shown. It can begin simply by loving the world God has made—an always awakening to the spaciousness of daylight, the passion of colors, the touch of winds, the motion of birds. It culminates surely in a great kindness toward all men; because every man is God's, named by God and with a purpose and a meaning given him by God. So the heart's love toward God encompasses all that Jesus said about feeding the hungry, clothing the naked, visiting the sick and the prisoner. This is not a matter of duty. It is a way of returning God's endless love for us.

Come, Creator; come, Lord Jesus Christ; come, Holy Spirit!—be in us and browse in us this day. Be in us power to love. Be in us mercy for the broken heart, and healing for the broken bones, and grace for the day's journey. Be in us silence for listening to all the bells and truths of heaven in our midst. Flow in us like our blood. Cling to us like our flesh. Surround us like the air. And let our prayers come unto thee forever. Amen.

O Lord, find in us those places where we truly repent and receive the confession of our hearts for we have wounded the innocent, betrayed the just, denied the true, and destroyed the holy. Make our sorrow real, our intention valiant, our return steady. And whether we stand firm against the evils in us, or falter and fall again; hold us in the enormous hands of thy mercy, and re-create us in the image of thy joy; through Jesus Christ our Lord. Amen.

The day comes on shining. Azures are everywhere. Earth stirs. Kitchens and palaces, valleys and belfries, lands and cities, awake, awake! The Lord reigneth. He gives us the swirl and the sun, the bread and the hope. He gives us this day. It is he who handles all space as a very little thing and puts the stars to flight. Praise him, for he is our Lord and holy is his name. Amen.

"Thou shalt love God with all thy mind . . ."

There are various ways of describing the mind in us. In one way, the mind is a gatherer, a sort of beachcomber, picking up and storing a variety of facts, ideas, memories. Its fingers are our five—or more—senses. But the mind can—usually—take what it gathers up and sort it out and put it in place. Here the mind is an organizer and a reasoner. The mind is also a skeptic—if it wants to be. It asks questions of its information; it asks embarrassing questions that annoy the heart and upset faith. Yet the mind is basically the blend of both the heart and faith. It is just as possible to speak of the passionate mind as to speak of the passionate heart; and it is just as possible for the mind to serve God passionately as for the heart. In fact, mind and heart—and soul—depend on one another. The whole man is these three working—with the body—as one. How rightly the command of Jesus is to love God with all our mind. But, of course, we need to inquire what this requires of us.

O God, may the praises of your house come from the bones you knitted into us, arise in the hearts which you gave us for life and love, speak from the minds which wear the colors of your freedom. For we walk and run and kneel by your grace. We love, because you first loved us; and we shall delight who freely choose in all things to glorify your name. Amen.

Dear Lord, the sin of man is contagious. It is in us all. It darkens us against thy light. It fevers us before thy calm. It knots in us and aches in us as we hear thy truth. Surely we cannot heal ourselves. O thou whose forgiveness brims over all the world and whose mercies are the medicines that make all things well, forgive us this day, and let thy mercies cleanse us soul, bone, and blood; through Jesus Christ. Amen.

For the daylight open upon us; for the air's tall breath that comrades beside us and is a lover within us; for the visible ceremonies of the seasons and the invisible dances of the heart; for the surgery of fearless minds and the healing of compassionate hands; for suffering's wisdom and sorrow's strength; and for thyself, present and lively, among all sorts and conditions of men: we give our clamorous thanks. Amen.

"Thou shalt love the Lord thy God with all . . . thy soul."

The soul is the center of our meeting place with God. It is the holiness within us. It is a condition of being ready for God in the hour of his coming. It is that within us that encompasses us flesh and blood, mind and heart, with the felt sense that we belong to an order of being beyond this life of clocks and appointments, of minutes and years, and finally of death. Yet the soul is not separate from the body. In a way, the soul can be described as God incarnate in us, God made flesh, heaven clamped to the bones. Perhaps, we can say that the soul is who we really are as God sees us.

Thus, the soul's love for God is not a piecemeal, leftover wave of the pious hand to God. It is a dense, thick, fulsome adoration offered by all that we are. It is the kneeling of the whole man. It is the praise of the senses, the heart, the mind, the tongue, the hands, the silence, the anguish, the joy. It is the concentration of the grace of God within us.

January Fourth Sunday

Lord, in whose large and endless light all darknesses are held; by whose command airs march, days arise, and seasons come and go; whose mercies encircle us and whose joys invite us: come to our worship. Be in us light, command, mercy, and joy. Enter us so that our hands shall pray thee, and our tongues sing thee, and our ears hear thee, and souls desire thee. For we gather before thee in our brokenness; and it is thyself alone can make us whole. Amen.

O God, we are sorry for what we are: for the meanness in us like little knives, for the envy in us like little spiders, for the self-pity in us like bleating sheep, for the gossip in us like noisy sparrows. For these small daily sins and for the large sins whereby we injure the peace of the world and turn our households and ourselves away from thee, we pray thy forgiveness. Yea, Lord, without thee we are but broken pieces of men. In thy mercy, mend us, and give us over to the uses of love; through Jesus Christ our Lord. Amen.

Yea Lord, Sovereign over us, Savior redeeming us, Spirit surrounding us: we give thee our body's adoration, our heart's thanksgiving, and our soul's continuous praise. For thou hast sung the heavens, written the seasons, and set the staves of stars. Thou hast made us, molded us, consoled us, and redeemed us. Thou hast turned our hands to build peace and hast taught our feet the dances of eternity. O marvelous are thy conversations, and holy is thy name. Praise be to Father, Son, and Holy Ghost. Amen.

January

Fifth Sunday

Jesus pictured the kingdom of heaven in many simple ways using a wheat field, a grain of mustard seed, a buried treasure, and so on; he also chose some wild and mysterious images—"The kingdom of God is like lightning in the sky—lo here! lo there!" But we understand him most when he likens the kingdom of heaven to children—the laughing, dancing, noisy, wild, and tender children that have peopled the earth since the beginning of mankind—the kittens of the world. Strangely, we who were once children and, therefore, of the order of the kingdom of heaven, have a hard time remembering how it was being a child—full of wonder, full of grace, and, to be sure, sometimes overfull with tears. Yet most of us still have enough of some original joy that we can be, perhaps, most joyous when a child tosses a ball in the air or turns a somersault or laughs at the trees—gifts that we are given that we cannot earn or pay for. But even when our children do not behave as "a little lower than the angels," we love them, labor for them, beat out our very hearts for them as well as our bank accounts—or so it seems. In the maelstrom of this present age, however, all is not well for children or with children. We have deluged them with things, with education, with trips abroad, with a scientific civilization second to none, with open doors to affluence greater than our own. Yet as our joy has gone from us, so has theirs. Have we given them our love by putting second things first?

Almighty God, we praise thee for the night gone by, that thou kept us in safety and renewed us in sleep. We praise thee for this day's rising and its thousand new beginnings. We praise thee for thy presence in the congregation, for thy Word proclaimed, for thy grace in our prayers, for holy worship lively in our bones. We praise thee for thyself who made us, for thy Son who saved us, and for thy Spirit which enlivens us. Glory to God in the highest. Amen.

O Lord, in whose mystery abide the world and all its sundry peoples and on whose compassion rest the hopes and fears of all men ever born, thy glory astonishes us. Before thy majesty we are meager sons and daughters. Evil is on our tongues. We play at faith. We serve thee casually as it pleases our comfort; and, even as Adam, hide from thee when thy searching finds us out. O Lord, ransack the little ordered rooms of our dignity and spill us out into wide and dangerous weathers of our deepest needs; and there receive us in thy mercy until we are wholly thine; through Jesus Christ our Lord. Amen.

O God, this day we praise thee with our singing voices and our new blue robes and our washed faces. We lift up sopranos of rejoicing for white ski slopes and football games and chocolate cake and large, friendly dogs. We have glad songs for thy love that watches over all the world and cares for all people. Had we drums and cymbals, we would strike them loud for thy laughter everywhere in us and around us; and we pray that there will always be music in us, whether we are young or old, to sing in the days of sadness and to remember by and to give our thanksgivings unto thee; through Jesus Christ our Lord. Amen.

It is God himself who affirms the world and all people. The dry land, airs, oceans, space in its vastest reaches—all are his, fashioned (who knows how) in the divine mystery. And man is God's, from Adam even unto ourselves—all people formed in the divine image, all of us partaking of eternity from the moment of our first breath. Nature and man are both affirmed by God and in God; yet both nature and man have fallen away from God. "All we have gone astray like lost sheep, we have turned everyone to his own way," runs the Confession. The whole creation travaileth and groaneth for deliverance, writes Paul. We are in God and of God; but something has gone amiss, awry, evilly wrong. We are in God, but we turn from God. In fact, we are in a time when man—despite much pious verbiage—lives his life without God, or so he assumes. This is sin. It is also death. For, if we cut ourselves off from God, we sever our tie with the source of all life. We become broken branches, dried-up streams, empty vessels. Yet in his largess, in his mercy, God still holds us, though we do not feel his hands.

Almighty God, by whose strength the earth leans toward its sun and by whose mercies the nations shall arise in peace and go forth in joy: center us down in thyself that we may offer thee true worship; and receive whatever in us, great or small, worthily shows thee adoration; through Jesus Christ our Lord. Amen.

Almighty God, the days come more burdened than we can bear, and sadness lingers in us like winter, and we know our sin. We live in a turning away from thee, and we falter and fall in broken promises and empty dreams. O God, even our words go empty before thee. We pray thy Mercy, thy Strength, and thy Forgiveness to cleanse us, to straighten our souls, and to set us free. Hear us and save us. Amen.

O God, thou art over all: the stars that burn against the spaces, the mountained and the valleyed earth, the trade winds racing on the oceans, snow at the wintertide, the dark leaping rain, cities awake, and love alive in a thousand thousand houses. All are thine. And everyman is thine: his breath, his blood, his bone, his start, his journey, his arrival. Praise! Amen.

February — Second Sunday

There is a great, sad cry that speaks out of the heart of the Christian faith: "Woe to the double-minded!" It is an awesomely realistic cry, for it describes man as he usually is—a being somehow desiring to be in the presence of God; yet, more frequently than not, a being who turns away from God to deal with the world on strictly human terms. To be double-minded is to try to worship both God and mammon; it is to engage in a hundred-and-one-small idolatries and, at the same time, to affirm the truth of the First Commandment: "Thou shalt have no other gods before me." But the way to God is to have "the single eye," which means, amazingly and necessarily, to have a chastity of concern for God, to look for God in all experience, to have a purity of mind and heart that returns all that happens in a day or a lifetime to be resolved for its meaning in the counsels of God. Perhaps, the guilt that all of us live with—the deep, unpenetrated guilt we all bear for the world's sorrows and man's inhumanity to man—is in us because we live double-mindedly. We are chained to the world yet long to be free in the delight that we know when we center ourselves and our purposes, urgently and finally, down in God himself.

February — Second Sunday

O God, beyond language there is thy Word; beyond sin there is thy Holiness; beyond fear there is thy Love. Thou art the Breath that breathes us; thou art the Hand that holds us; thou art the Heart that loves us. Go with us this day and all days, almighty and redeeming Lord. Amen.

Hear our confession, gracious Lord; and in thy mercy, pardon and revive us. Behold us a comfortable people, neither hot nor cold toward thy love; neither affirming thee nor denying thee; having purposes but not thy purpose; working our works but not thy work; acting on truths but not thy truth. So we come somewhere but still are nowhere. So we live gracefully without grace. Great Lord, defend us from our goodness, our successes, and our ease. Root us in dense and holy depths that we may have life and life abundantly. Amen.

O come, let us praise the Lord, who made us all. He has sustained us day by day; he has delivered us from sin and death. He is the depth under all depths; he is the height above all heights. Because he is, we are. At our beginning he is our breath and hope; and at our end he is our health and salvation. O come, let us praise the Lord. Amen.

February — Third Sunday

It may be that some future generation will describe us as the people who lost their desire for the vision of God. Not many of us are troubled by Jesus' words, "No man has ever seen God." We concur with this observation with the greatest of ease, because we live in a culture that does not take God seriously and among peoples who have lost their sense of awe. We do not expect to see God. We are not sure we would want to see God, if we could. We are not like men and women of an earlier time for whom the very passion of life was to behold God face to face. The saint's discipline that led him toward the "beatific vision" finds no place in the order of our living. We desire no Holy Grail. Even the Reformers' description of the purpose of man's life—"to glorify God and to enjoy him forever"—has become for us little more than an ancient, if not quaint, saying. All this apathy in us is most pitiful. It is the very marrow of our tragedy as people. It is the reason we are stunted in soul, crippled at heart, a people who limp through the daylight and crouch in the nights. For what we need most is to behold God, to be caught up in his beauty and his presence.

February — Third Sunday

Come, Holy Spirit, find our hearts. Brood in our flesh, in the stretch of our muscles, in our fingertips. Be like air surrounding us that we may taste and touch the holy things and know the great gladness of our Lord Jesus Christ. Be in our prayers, O mysterious One, that we may desire thee with a complete desire. Amen.

O Lord, with what words can we come who in our thoughts and acts have set ourselves against you? Can you pity our vanity? Can you be patient with the lukewarm? Can you forgive us who are afraid to dream dreams and to see visions? Can you love us as we are? For, except we are in you, we are a vain and muttering noise, a dull people, a lost generation. Save us, most merciful Father. Amen.

Thou art breath: and the air marches, the clouds go and cease, the lungs fill, the flesh dances. Thou art hands: and the morning stars abide, the vast daylight holds in place, the broken cities are mended, and the living and the dying are cradled forever. Thou art mystery: and in thee is hidden wonder; the other side of dark is thine; and the brown sparrow in the eaves is comrade to thy lightning. Glory and honor and majesty and power are thine forever and ever. Amen.

February — Fourth Sunday

We are in a time of mobility, a time of to-and-fro, a time when it is part of our agony as well as our pleasure not to find a resting-place or a fixed purpose. We need a center, but our days seem to fly off in a thousand unrelated directions. We want a harbor, a place of return; but our senses are more intrigued by the ships that sail away. We are constantly in motion, not only outwardly after all the world's prizes, but inwardly we are churning with the ancient anxieties of our loves, our angers, and our mortality. Such is our turmoil that we are not quite sure whether we even belong to ourselves. So much of what we are and do seems spurious; because, though we go in haste, we do not arrive significantly anywhere. When St. Augustine soberly and joyously declared, "Our hearts are restless until they find their rest in thee," he spoke out of the experiences of a life that literally had been on the run trying out one pleasure after another—only to arrive nowhere. He discovered that it is God alone who makes sense out of our motion, who gives meaning to the race. If we must run, let us run toward eternity.

February — Fourth Sunday

O thou who made light and earth, water and air; thou who shaped within man's flesh a radiant soul; thou who saviored all things made in Jesus Christ: surround and invade us with thy Spirit, till we behold thy whole creation and are made glad by thy goodness set within us. Then, turn us to receive thy blessing upon our work and thy strength upon our purposes. Amen.

O Lord, gracious and good and forever abiding, how can you suffer us, your lukewarm people, who toward your sweet persuasions blow neither hot nor cold? How can you wait upon us who will not turn, who will not turn to you for love, and so from fear to trust, from sin to grace, from death to endlessness? How can you bear with us who day by day go indolent before you? O shake us down to earth! And, then, by mercy's blows enliven us to live toward you; and bend our flesh to adoration and our souls to praise; through Jesus Christ our Lord. Amen.

We praise the Lord, who is our Father eternally, who fashioned the earth and the glory upon it, who cast the circle of the sky and set out the luminous squares of light and dark, who is the air's master and the chemist of the waters and the fire, who takes our flesh and informs it with a soul, who for our sakes surprises death and takes us unto himself forever. Amen.

March — First Sunday

When we speak of a man's salvation, we are concerned with what he amounts to . . . eternally. Even to wonder about salvation is to affirm that there is within us a need, an insistence to possess or to be possessed by a destiny which is nobler than what we apparently are from day to day. Salvation places us squarely before our mystery and asks, "Who are you?" and "Where are you going?" and "Where will you arrive?" Yet in our present age—so long as the lawns are mowed and the salary large enough and the trinkets lovely enough—we leave eternity to the professionals, somewhat amused that even they should take eternity and salvation with such awesome seriousness. And yet salvation is ultimately involved with all in our living that gives us joy rather than mere pleasure, dense and rich wonder rather than mere curiosity, honest and full understanding rather than mere haphazard guesswork. The Bible, that great, holy, solid, unread book, centers us down on salvation; steadily sets forth who man really is; and bespeaks to each man, who will hear and hold on, the deeps and heights which are the Way of his salvation.

March — First Sunday

O Lord, by whose love fear vanishes, by whose forgiveness sin falls away, and by whose mercy our mortality is overcome: come to us, fearful, sinful, and mortal. By love persuade us; by forgiveness heal us; and by mercy resurrect us. Let thy Word avalanche against our pretending; help our prayers speak out of our deepest need; awaken us to man's distresses; and keep us strong in trust toward thee; through Jesus Christ who is thyself revealed. Amen.

O God, we have foundered in the darkness, fought the demons, and lost. We drag in the chains of fear linked upon fear. We are broken with self-punishment. Come to us now as we are—frail and human and most miserable—and let the love of Jesus Christ brood in our hearts, until we know—as thou hast always told us—that thy forgiveness is given seventy times seven and even forever. Amen.

O God, we praise you for the people who accept us with all of our frailties. We praise you for the men who do not have to win all of the time. We praise you for the critics who speak eye-to-eye and person-to-person. We praise you for the sinners who do not thank you that they are not as other men. We praise you for Jesus Christ who lost most of the battles and for the Holy Ghost whose speech is often incoherent. We praise you for yourself, that you are there for us when the fearful ones run away. Amen.

March — Second Sunday

There is no geography, however spacious, unchartered, dangerous, or majestic, as the landscape which is man. His dimensions are as unfathomed as the space that lies outside him; his territories are as limitless as the oceans and lands that surround him; his measure is as unexplored as the Amazon; and his height and depth are Everests that have not yet been climbed. Yet, at the same time, he is "the chaff that the wind driveth away," "a flower of the field" that fadeth and is soon cut down. He perpetuates himself by the hand's cunning that turns stone into statues and steel into skyscrapers; he writes his name in bold paintings and humming factories; he engages in poems and novels to tell himself of his own meaning, sending his love to the heavens and his compassion out across all mankind. Yet, at the same time, his most striking monuments often are barbarian acts of war, as caught in uncontrollable lusts of power and safety, he seeks to destroy himself.

He balances precariously between two questions: "What is man?" and "What is man that thou art mindful of him?" His place in his own cosmic geography, his meaning as he stands before his monuments, depend on which question he asks and what answer he receives.

March — Second Sunday

Forasmuch, dear Lord, as this day is given, and our hearts brim with breath, and our bodies are lively with new strength, and all that we are gathers gladly to thy rising, so we rejoice and praise thee forever. Thou hast arched a sky over us, thou hast sent winds, thou hast awakened in us a dance, and thou hast set thy music in our very souls. Glorious is thy name. Amen.

O God, we confess we do not want to confess the fault in us. We abandon you day by day, more by more, year by year. We like you best bland, buttery, and harmless. We prefer you as zero. O as we dance to our polkas of pride and strut to the four-quarter beat of our wars, break up our gamesmanship, put to rout our neat line of march, and toss us pell-mell in the whirl and agony of our sin—where we may be crushed and know that you are God. Amen.

Wondrous God, your daylight opens upon us hope, good labor, new joys. We live because of you, and we are alive in you. You make for each of us a way among all various ways; and whether we take the path of ease, sorrow, burden, laughter, foolishness, or wisdom, you are on the way with us. You make blessed all the days of our lives. Amen.

Think now what a marvel it is to be born a man, what it is to be this intricate cluster of bone and flesh and running tides of blood and system of radar, what it is to have at one's bidding five senses—five to-and-fro messengers who bring us news of the day and world and odors and stinging sweet tastes and landscapes and music beyond language and the easy and hard touch of surfaces and depths. Say what it is to be a man among men—a mystery among mysteries—a gathering of hope, a center of dreaming all mingled in with pain and sorrow and dying.

It is this man we bring to the church for a conversation with the eternal God. It is this self who does not ever quite know who he is that we venture to stand in the presence of the Lord who made heaven and earth—to hear the ultimate abiding Word, to seek the Light that opens up the darkness, to ask for the Life that makes all life alive.

O Lord, our very silence is exclamation when we meditate on thy glory, when our eyes see inwardly thy form over all things, when our ears hear the tread of thy love on our streets, when our tongues taste thy goodness, when our whole being knows the sweet and the rough of thy coming and going upon us. Our words cry out, and our songs arise, and our hearts uplift, and our souls follow after thee. Amen.

Vast God, because we are men not gods, we bring to our world our frailty as well as our wisdom. Our touch upon the earth has a blemish. Our faith has its doubt; our hope has its fear; our strength has its weakness. Here we confess ourselves to be ourselves and little more, except thy power sustains us and thy love renews us. O thou who comest to all men in Jesus Christ our Lord, forgive us for what we are and make us thine. Amen.

Most sovereign Lord, we gather in thy praise. Our ten fingers are thy workmen; our feet in trudge or race are thine errand men; our ears wait upon thy Word; and our eyes look up to thy glory. The heart is thy hammering place and the mind thy schoolhouse. We are held in thy mercy, made alive in thy mystery, and satisfied in thy grace. Our tongues be thy instruments, thy praise, forever and ever. Amen.

"Man," writes Karl Barth, "does not seek for solutions but for salvation." Herein Barth gathers up the whole intention of the Bible and quietly asserts our actual human situation as it is any time in history. We look at ourselves every day on the pages of a newspaper, in the shadows speaking on the television set, in the pantomimes that take place in schools, factories, and even in churches. We see ourselves. We see man simultaneously eager for life and then bored by its monotonies, violent in war yet earnest for peace, disciplined to pursue bread for his body yet chaotic and lazy in finding food for his soul—always a paradox beset by demons and angels.

As we see ourselves, read about ourselves, listen to our own wisdom, we encounter from all sides the language of solution—a perennial patching up of the world's brokenness by each generation. And as we bandage up our wounds, put splints on the fractures, take various political and scientific aspirin to calm the pain—in our hearts we and all men long for the healing that is wholeness and holiness and fullness—long, indeed, for salvation!

O God, you made us lively and bold, a framework of bones and a flesh of paradise and pain. You set the furnace of the heart and the slow-and-quick fires of the blood. You awakened in us a soul and proposed the mind's adventure. Daily we live in you, and by grace may we live for you. O make in us a sounding praise forever. Amen.

Lord of hosts, the havoc of evil is in us all. The storms of the ancient sins tremble in our blood and terror in our hearts. Lust and anger, greed and pride, and gluttony we do confess. Yet worse, we confess the doldrum sins: our cliché righteousness, our easy winking at the lie, our adoration of the stupid, our sneer at grace, our boredom with eternity. O God, send us the true calm of mercy and redeem us in the lively weather of love; through Jesus Christ our Lord. Amen.

In thee, great God, the twisted things are straightened, the crippled are enlivened and made whole, blindmen see, and the slain arise in resurrection. In thee the tired ones shall run, the angered ones speak peace, and those tangled in darkness shall declare the light. In thee shall everyman know the time of his rejoicing. Yea, unto thee be our praise—our shouting praise—our cries of gladness—this day and even forever. Amen.

April — First Sunday

The redemptive or healing power of the church at any time in the world's history will depend ultimately upon the faith of its saints—that is, upon the few or many who seriously and joyfully put their trust in God's faithfulness toward man. They believe that God's promises will be fulfilled, that, over against all men's sin and nature's evil, God's mercies shall prevail. The saint by his faith, his trust, knows that salvation, God's victory and man's redemption, is at hand, is now, is in this moment; and this being so—no one need fear life or death ever again. Every night is Christmas Eve and every dawn is Easter, because Jesus Christ dies for us and with us on every Good Friday.

The saints' faith moves where the mysteries of God and man are truly revealed and where the sadnesses and pain of mortal life are illuminated and transformed, because faith knows that our God holds us surely and tenderly forever. Our modern churches, spawning out, building, busy, organizing, counting, competing, and so rarely different from the world surrounding them, would do well to ponder Jesus' words: "When the Son of man comes, shall he find faith?"

April *First Sunday*

In thee, O God, we begin who never were, except in thee. By thee, we go our way and touch and know the green world, the air's music, the sadnesses of joy, the strength of sorrow, love's hands and voices, the wordless mysteries of mercy given and received. In thee we end, and in the end arise in thee, forever; through Jesus Christ our Lord. Amen.

O God, Searcher of hearts, you know who we are: that we are fitful and lazy in our devotion to that which is holy; that we are embarrassed in the presence of that which is pure; that we are fearful and slow in acceptance of that which is true. You know us: that we can carry hate in our hearts, evil on our tongues, greed in our hands. You know that there is a warfare within us. Give us, O God, your peace that the storms within may be stilled. Amen.

O God, we praise you for the small, diminished things: for the health at the edge of our sicknesses, for the moment's quiet in the hours of storm, for the few that held when the many broke and ran, for an answer of love in a lynch mob of hate, for the honest saint in a city of betrayals. We praise you for the minor key, the oblique kindness, the hidden joy. May Jesus Christ understand us in whose name we pray. Amen.

The religious life can wear pretty thin. The liturgies of the church can grow stale; the perpetual strain of being called to do good works can utterly weary us. Prosperity itself can offer enough amusements so that we can turn from the disciplines of faith and apparently feel little loss. And, conversely, adversities can so overwhelm us that we become victims of our own bitterness—so much so that the usual routines of religion hardly meet our need. So faith droops and grows tired; the exultations give way to boredom with all things ecclesiastical.

Somehow, somewhere along the way, we have lost touch with the reality of God, and the symbols and the words which point to him are not enough. It is at such a desperate time, in such a dry and empty season, that the soul of man must be fed and renewed at the deep levels, must be reacquainted with the sources, must confess its weakness and call mightily and seriously with the psalmist: "My soul thirsteth for thee, my flesh longeth for thee in a dry and thirsty land."

April Second Sunday

Almighty God, enter with light this time of our worship. Be as the morning to our dark and as a fair day to our fears. Surround us with thine overarching love. Warm us with forgiveness for each other. Ready us for the wounds that we must bear, and enliven us with such a trust in thee that our prayers may be honest and our lives put to the uses of joy; through Jesus Christ our Lord. Amen.

O God, in the world's rage we watch and wait, aware of our weakness, worried by our guilt. Evil is in us and around us. Our faith is tired and our wills enfeebled by our fears. Give us strength. Arouse us by love. Turn our hands to compassion, our minds to reason, and our hearts to trust. We beseech thee; in Jesus' name. Amen.

O blessed Lord, thou hast given us earth and life, the rivers of water, roads crisscross on a thousand hills, the hands' five and cunning fingers, and the eyes we love. Praise be to thee forever and ever! Thou hast taught us the ways of sorrow, the anger of pain, the sadness of time. Praise be to thee forever and ever. Thou hast taken us, molded us, held us, consoled us, and saved us. Thou hast killed our death. Thou hast given us heaven. Praise be to thee, our God, forever and ever. Amen.

April — Third Sunday

There is a time when faith wavers, when it stumbles, when it falls. And, perhaps, if this were not so, faith could not be faith; for even the practices of love toward family, toward neighbors, toward God, weary us. The goodwill of love dries up, and we become angered by the clichés of goodness itself. Or we look out on the world and, with envy in our hearts, seem to see the shining prizes given to the incompetent and the triumphs fall to the hosts of wickedness. Days come when bitterness eats away in us over the pain we cannot cure and the chaos we cannot set right again.

It is here in the dry and empty places of the soul's defeat that we are to learn the deeps and the joys, the mysteries and the glories, of the devout life. It is here that prayer is neither an embarrassment for reasonable men nor a set of formulas for lazy and sentimental men. Here we can be led to the true uses of silence, to the necessities of trust, and to the felt reality of every prayer lifted up on behalf of other men.

April — Third Sunday

Almighty God, you have returned us from the long marches of sleep; you have summoned us from our separate darknesses; you have called us into the daylight. In you alone we hope. Let our prayers come unto you, fragile and bewildered and broken though they be, until our falsehood tangles with your truth and our vanity is shaken by your power. Bring us through this day, restless for your peace within our hearts and for your righteousness plain within our souls. Amen.

O God, the infection of sin is in us all, and we are weak with the maladies of little prides and little hates and little fears. Our faith has a palsy, our hope a paralysis, and our love a chill; and for too long we have tranquilized our sick souls on pink pills and barley water. Be surgeon to us, and with the knife of your grace cut us to the marrow, and with the medicines of your mercy make us whole; through Jesus Christ our Lord. Amen.

Lord, in this day also shall your eternity be given, and we shall breathe your large air and live; and amid the push and the haul, the rising and the falling, the anger and the kindness, we shall learn again that you are God. So every day is gift; every love is gift; every hope is gift. O praise, all praise! You give yourself over and over and over, forever and ever. Amen.

Palm Sunday

The Palm Sunday procession says to us as much or little as we are ready to hear or to see. Perhaps, it is mostly a glad cry that somehow God is quietly going by on our street—an event that is, indeed, cause for hosannas! God on a donkey reminds us, too, of some words of Paul that say, "The foolishness of God is wiser than man"; and we wonder what this "foolishness" is trying to say. Why does God in Jesus Christ march on a city, the holy city Jerusalem, in a parade more like that of children than of a conqueror? We think of St. Francis preaching to the birds, of the child in the manger, Alyosha, Galahad, all the innocent ones who give a shining to the world's heavy dark. The word describing the event is "blessed." Something is happening here that the hearts of men long for. Is it the desire to be restored to innocence and trust? Is it a hope that we can again laugh spontaneously? Is it the vast longing in all men for peace that is more than armed truce? Is it conscience speaking to indifference? Hear, then, this quiet parable for your soul's refreshment.

Palm Sunday

O God, come to us this day in the parable of the meek king. Lift up our eyes always to the green tree. Give us the patience for burden and sadness of the small beast. Quicken us to the hidden laughter. Surprise us by joy. And against our walled cities, our regiments of fear, our committees of pride—let the children come, and the dances of trust, and the somersaults of hope. Let the meek king be heard. Amen.

Gentle Lord, on this day which celebrates your simplicities, we confess that we have been overly in love with pomp and circumstance and all the noisy glories and prizes of this world. We have goose-stepped to the drums of war, danced to the pipers of prestige, skipped to the spring songs of security. O we who are lulled by the big lie and the mammoth stupidities pray for your mercy. Give us honest eyes to see the falsehoods that beset us, and turn us again to Jesus Christ who redeems all things by quiet victories. Amen.

Blessed is he who bids our pride fall to its knees, who awakens our households to joy, who shines the vast sun of his love on the streets of our fears. Blessed is he who shows us the patient world and brings peace to the cities of wrath. Blessed is the quiet Word of the Lord. Blessed is he who builds up the waste places and gives his life for all the people. Hosanna in the highest. Amen.

Good Friday

The irony of being simply men and women—and not gods or heroes—is that we seem to hear the deep awesome ring of life only in the catastrophe, the war, the death. The days of peace, when calm and ease are upon us, find us indifferent, casual bystanders almost unaware and often unthankful for the abundance that we have. Socrates has to drink the hemlock to persuade us the true purpose of life is the education of the soul. Jesus cries out, "Jerusalem, Jerusalem, which stoneth the prophets," and goes to the cross; only then do men take him seriously. The nonviolent, huge-hearted men who come among us with compassion and laughter and trust—these we send out of our cities and towns as we invite in Caesar and Napoleon, bolster up our insurance policies, and keep the strangers out. We send the nonchalant, laughing, generous men away —the apostles who speak for the spacious nature of man and the sacredness of life; we send them into exile or to death; and with them, unwittingly, we send our consciences and our joy. Martin Luther King is dead, and now we will hear him. We will let his compassion come rolling in upon us. His call for justice—always coupled with mercy—will command us. Because of him our consciences will return to make us men again; and his buoyancy, his excitement over life, his dream for America will be in us; and some of our lost joy will come home. Pray, then, that conscience and joy will lead us to enact in our bodies—as he did—compassion and justice in the streets of our land.

Good Friday

O Lord, sometimes the very light in us is darkness. We stumble about in the blindness of our own conceits. We trip over our pride. We do not see . . . but worse, we do not want to see. And many times we are afraid to show mercy, to act out compassion, to cry out to one another our forgiveness and our love. O may Jesus Christ, who did forgive the thief on the cross and show mercy to all sorts of miserable men and teach us that love like faith overcomes mountains, come to us this day and be in us and make us alive and whole again. Amen.

Hear, mighty Lord, how with one voice we speak our sorrow for our sins, those darknesses within us that we set between ourselves and thee. O we are creatures of the little prides, the lazy mind, the meager trust, and the envious heart. The muddled world that we fear is our own monster. We are matted in by stupidities and nighted in by blindness. Take us now, thou majestic and merciful One, and teach us the hard lesson of forgiveness. Let the Love we deny save us; through Jesus Christ our Lord. Amen.

O God, we sin and add to the world's misery. Given each other to love, and all mankind to hope for, and thyself to trust, we are too busy for love, too anxious for hope, and too proud to trust. Because of us, because of us, great Lord, the four pale horsemen ride—famine, war, pestilence, and death. By thy mercy, forgive us and all men for what we do to one another. Deliver us from the shame of ourselves, and turn us again and again to spend our lives on the world's sorrow; through Jesus Christ our Lord. Amen.

Easter Sunday

Across the world with bells and carols, ancient words and prayers rooted in the history of Western man, we declare that Christ has risen from the dead and that death shall have no dominion over us. The Christian community that makes this announcement is presently ill at ease over this very declaration, because many both outside and within the household of faith warn us that we should be spending more of our substance and energy on this world and its anguish and far less on talking about the next. What these critics set aside far too casually is that it makes a difference in the way we live within the world whether we view man as a sophisticated but ultimately trapped animal or a person whose being and meaning always have eternal references. At the very least, Easter presses upon us the questioning of what *in the world* we exist by and for. One side of Easter is surely our death, the psalmist's cry that "our days are like grass." The other side takes us into the very presence of God, reaffirms every inkling and intimation that comes to us in living that we belong within a grace that holds us forever. Now, as across the world multitudes assemble and bells and anthems shake out to the skies, we hear our own voices declaring: "Death, thou too shall die!" And we stand with everyman as he finds himself aware that he wears the colors of eternity.

Easter Sunday

Thou who art creator above us and savior among us, we come acknowledging thy majesty of airs around us for breath and delight, of cloud-capped days and the tall nights coming down with stars, of seasons and tongue-tastes and canticles of winds and birds and trees; and we come praising thy Mystery of mercy—Jesus Christ our Lord— who offers us love for fear, healing for brokenness, truth for fraud, depth for surfaces, brimming hope for emptiness, resurrection for death. Glory and honor, dominion and power are thine forever and ever. Amen.

O God, how can we come before thee in sin who so rarely approach thee in adoration? O the wrong in us is great! We have been busy with the art of self-pity, the enjoyment of our angers, the feeding of our prejudices. We have wasted our days and dreaded our nights. We feel baffled, troubled at heart, and useless. Turn us now from the tangle and the idolatry to a plain path, to a trust in thee; and transform us by the steady arm of thy forgiveness into new men validly alive in all times and places because we are alive in thee; through Jesus Christ our resurrected Lord. Amen.

Praise be to thee, O sovereign and majestic Lord, for in our rising, thou art our strength; and in our going about, thou art our protector; and in our falling, thou art our deliverer. Though the air split with fire and the mountains of death arise around us, thou wilt redeem misery and all miserable men, thou wilt take away fear and all fearful men, thou wilt redeem death and all dying men. Praise be to thee. Amen.

May — First Sunday

It is an alarming business when we go about trying to understand who we are, we in the church, we who are the professing Christians in our generation; but, of course, it is a necessary task as more and more we look exactly like the society that is around us. With a becoming, though perhaps doubtful, humility the church has lately taken to calling itself the community of sinners. But this is not so much humility as truth-telling; it is not new insight but ancient history. On the other hand, we would do gloriously well to reaffirm another ancient but ever new description of the church as the community of the hopeful ones and the joyous ones. For we, among all men, have cause for hope, have cause for rejoicing in the God who delights in his created world; the God whose enormous and holy hands hold history and heaven together; the God who testifies in Jesus Christ, for the sake of all men, that "death shall be no more, neither shall there be mourning nor crying nor pain, for the former things have passed away." And for these causes which are the foundations of our faith, we are called "to be minstrels of the Lord," living in our world with jubilation and praise, at our daily work, eating our daily bread, and ministering to all sorts and conditions of men.

May — First Sunday

O God, our God, thou who hast awakened us from sleep into the new day, come even so with thy morning unto our soul's darkness and bring thy life unto our death, that in thee we may arise in light and go forth in mercy. Make us a music of rejoicing that we may truly praise thee; and so persuade us to thy presence in all things that we will move among the places of this world, seeing the motion of thy hands upon our work and feeling thee alive in every corner. Teach us to wear the hour as though it were eternity; through Jesus Christ our Lord. Amen.

O God, we do confess the punishment of our own sin: our hates whip us within, our fears keep us in chains, our pride prisons us. Yea, our sin is a lash, a manacle, a wall; and we are dungeoned in from the air of life and solitary from thy joy—except thy keys of forgiveness burst the locks and set us free again and again; through Jesus Christ our Lord. Amen.

Praise we now with glad hearts, with a minstrelsy of gladness, with tongues and eyes and hearts, gladsome and luminous and immense, our God, more immense than hearts, more luminous than eyes, more gladsome than tongues. For he is beyond our songs. He is lightning that eyes cannot dream; and he folds our prayers in his hands, making our little into his vast much. He is the watcher who broods over us and loves us from breath to breath. Even now he enjoys us. Even now he exclaims in us. Even now he prays our prayer. Amen.

In the praise of whatever you can praise, let the day begin. What you have of air—that air that rushes to your lungs and sends the blood through the trailways of your being, or that Maytime air that surrounds you like a blue bowl or touches your cheek or in your ear tells you what you did not know before or only half remember of some ancient joy—arrives as a gift. Then there is love. Give praise for it, for it does not come to you as wages earned or as a blue ribbon for winning the race. Something sings in a friend's heart toward you—who knows how or why?—and you are the beloved and the receiver. Even so forgiveness given in people's eyes or in the refreshment of a new day comes to us as though the Magi had knelt in our manger. True, the world wields around us and life falls upon us with agonies and fears and many falsehoods. But God, who is always in the midst of us, wears also the wound of our anguish and every hour redeems the losses and the horror by divine compassion. He is the Giver. Let the day begin in praise.

The day is given. Earth turns in the dark spaces. From its four corners the winds surge and sigh and race and rest. Birth cries, marriage rings, death tolls. The cities of men are beginning and growing and dying and ending. All is in God's hands. The day is given. Christ is risen. Praise the Lord. Amen.

O Lord, we approach thee for mercy; we come to be healed; we come for a vast forgiveness. For we stumble in the dark of our sins. We live with strange fears. We have a weariness that is heavy on us and in us. We are crippled seeking the things that do not satisfy, and we are not at peace with thee. Come now and overcome us; for only in thee is there health and a clear path, even Jesus Christ our Lord. Amen.

Almighty God, this cloud-capped world is thine; and the easy wide rivers, the green run of the winds, the cities of people, the daylights of understanding—all proclaim thee. Thy glory everywhere abounds, arises, and surrounds us. To thee belongeth all majesty, all honor, all power, and all praise; through Jesus Christ our Lord. Amen.

May — Third Sunday

One of the dancing words of the Christian faith is "grace." Grace being in a man, he comes alive; the gestures of his soul are not cliché; he awakens the routines to speak new thoughts and new dreams. He is, in essence, God's man—but not dolefully, heavily, or piously. Rather he has come to understand Jesus' words: "My yoke is easy and my burden is light." A man in grace is worth an army of men ponderously and prudently living by the ten commandments, because grace in him enlivens a man to a spontaneous goodness. God's love brims over in him and spills shiningly into the highways and byways of his living. The "grace-full" man does not deny or avoid evil, suffering, sin, or death; but he knows in his bones that "nothing can separate us from the love of God." We ought in the community of the church to pray first that we become grace-filled men and women. True it is that grace comes as a gift like air, light, laughter, love. It seizes us; we do not seize it. Yet grace is always being given. It visits us daily. Here we understand how Jesus wept over Jerusalem because she did not know the time of her visitation.

May — Third Sunday

Come, mighty Lord. Set thy daylight over all the earth; be sky in us. Bring again the furrow, flower, and green; plow in our hearts. Send whistlings and high calls among the treetops. Sing in our season. So may we live in grace, give love among men, and bring joy to the places of mourning. We beseech thee in the name of Jesus Christ, who is grace and love and joy. Amen.

O Lord, we move through thy world with a blurred vision, seeing it upside down, crooked, and contrawise. Pledged to self-interest, we make molehills into mountains and mountains into molehills. We set up the briar trees of self-pity and do not see the climbing forests of thy grace. O thou who art the true light that enlightens every man, keep us from stumbling in our own dark. Raise up our heads and open our eyes to see the landscapes of thy joy. Amen.

Daily and hourly and in this moment God's good and wholesome grace springs forth among us. God the Father gives it. Jesus Christ reveals it. The Holy Spirit bears it to us and to all men. Grace in us: angels dance in our blood, the lame walk, the sick are healed, the mountains rejoice, and the valleys are exalted. Now is the acceptable time. Now is the day of the Lord's favor. Glory be to Father, Son, and Holy Ghost. Amen.

We should not think otherwise than that the gospel intends us for joy. For joy we are born, for joy we live, and unto joy we die. For joy is not pleasure. Pleasure is, at most, a transient ecstasy; at least, it is a painless exercise; and, at worst, it produces a tiring monotony. Joy arises in the deep wellsprings of life where ecstasy is endless and clear and amazingly calm. Who goes with joy walks or runs, climbs or descends fearlessly—because he goes with God, in the serene yet ever-exciting joy of the Lord. Joy is participant in human happiness, but it is qualitatively more than human happiness. We can be happy over a child's innocence, a son's thoughtfulness, a friend's understanding. But joy arises in the God who gives innocence, awakens thoughtfulness, provides understanding. Joy is, moreover, the very watchword of the Gospels; it is the "good news"; it is the spontaneous power of the Christian man that spills over into love and compassion and adoration. Therefore, we only become niggardly and ridiculous when we trust God to the point of being dutiful in his name but not to the high and holy place of being joyful in his name as well.

O Magnificence around us, O Holiness above us, O Radiance within us: now is thy daylight upon us. Over the turning world thy winds advance. The cities waken one by one, the villages arise, and thy love talks in the squares. Thou art always the balance against our suffering. Thou art the trumpet of our peace. Blessed art thou, our Lord, forever and ever. Amen.

O God, we live not so much in light or dark as in the gray middle, the muddle, the meager, the half-felt, the half-known, the half-delighted-in. Not wanting joy, we are unprepared for sorrow; not accepting sorrow, we are unprepared for joy. Afraid of roots and depths, we have no tree, no height. O Lord, shake down the paper houses that we hide in and spill us out on the ground of thy strength. Unfasten us from fear, and set us free in trust. Undwarf our souls that we may come alive and grow within thy giant love; through Jesus Christ our Lord. Amen.

For whatever in us hears thee coming among us, stirring the season, sending the rains, moving the buds, running the robins—we rejoice and will rejoice, great Lord. For whatever in us sees thee going before us, breaking a new path, clearing a troubled mind, awaking a sleeping town, turning our purpose—we rejoice and will rejoice, good Lord. For whatever in us touches thee standing among us, shaping our prayers, healing our sick, breaking our evil, giving us vision—we rejoice and will rejoice, dear Lord. Praise is in us. Magnify that praise. Amen.

May

Fifth Sunday

We who feel in our bodies the presence of God—the brooding Spirit who warmly awakens us to the day, the One who presses the universe against us, the Breath that breathes in us our true calm, our true joy—we who are tangibly caught in God's net can "hope for what we do not see" and "wait for it with patience." We live *knowing* that despite all the anguish, anger, absurdity, loss, loneliness, and stark terror—all is well for man in God. But we cannot say this lightly or easily for other men; we can only speak for ourselves. Perhaps, we cannot even testify; because where war falls upon a people, when law and justice seem in conflict, when age and youth think themselves at odds—the praise of God can sound like evasion of the world's agony. But we can hope; and we can live within our hope; and by our hope we can heal, though we do so without fanfare. Because we can hope, we can believe in other men. We can engage in listening to what the other side says. We can, in our hope, see the signs of hope that arise in small events. We can in hope keep our heads—our "cool"—when voices are crying out for reprisals and punishments. In hope we can love our country and all its people, and we can send our hope across the spinning earth.

May

Fifth Sunday

Lord, the large heavens, this day, the countless families of man, are given by thy mercy and sustained by thy power; and all is well that this hour dwells in thee. So be in us the speech and supplication of our prayers, and make in us a silence for thy Word to come and overcome us. Encourage us in the risks of compassion toward all men and toward one another. Teach us awe before the holy mysteries. Let us come to thee with confession, hear thee with reverence, and go into our world with joy; because thou art God and faithful unto us forever. Amen.

O God, we have sinned against heaven in thy sight. We have been clever rather than kind, respectable rather than real, practical rather than penetrating. We have played the cynic before holy things, and out of the poverty of our own vision scoffed at the riches of faith. O Lord, take our thin, little, meager, beaten, self-pitying souls and by thy grace give them substance and hugeness and generosity and victory and trust; through Jesus Christ our risen Lord. Amen.

Thou art hidden as in spaces we have never seen nor dreamt of. Praise be thy mystery, O God. Thou wast in the world in Jesus Christ as a fire in the flesh, a fellow sufferer in the body, a redeemer from death. Praise be thy salvation, O God. Thou art with us now in the Holy Spirit as an assurance against fear, as a hand that blesses and guides, as a seeing though we are blind, as a gladness deep in every sorrow. Praise be thy compassion, O God. Praise Father, Son, and Holy Ghost. Amen.

June *First Sunday*

Those who will read the Gospels with a clear and understanding heart will not be long in discovering what the Christian life is. Of course, it is one thing to see and another thing to do, but surely the beginning is to have before us the specifics which are given. Underlying whatever else is declared or identified as the Christian life is the startling message that God has broken into history and has spoken his divine Word, Jesus Christ, for the forgiveness, the health, and the wholeness of all men. In Jesus Christ, moreover, the only true life is lived. It is the true life, because it is a handling of life as God himself handles life. People and things are respected and loved in themselves and in their freedom. One lives in the felt knowledge of the forgiveness of God; and, therefore, even when one brings into life his own sin, he lives on the side of the great affirmations: releasing captives, giving sight to the blind, setting at liberty the oppressed, proclaiming the glory of the Lord in all experience. This is the true life and purpose for which every man is born.

June *First Sunday*

Yea, great Lord, as by thy power thou hast turned this earth away from the stars unto the daylight and as by thy mercy thou hast brought us through the night and sleep unto life and morning, now by thy grace enlighten us within as we gather to thy worship. Receive our prayers, though they be broken and unworthy. Put joy in our singing. Teach us to hear each other's loneliness and to extend the hands of love. So entangle thyself in our flesh and hearts and minds that we cannot forget thee at our work, in our houses, among our dreams. Keep us from the foolishness that denies thee on prosperous days. Amen.

Eternal God, take from us that sin by which we declare we have no sin. Make us sorry for all the ways we have wounded one another. Keep us penitent for our neglect of the world's suffering, for the sick we have not visited, for the hungry we have not fed, for the naked we have not clothed, for the prisoners we have not set free. Especially, deepen our sadness for not having loved enough the holy, the chaste, and the innocent. Humble us now in our darkness that we may make ready to receive thy Light, our Lord Jesus Christ. Amen.

For all variety: bright, dark, sweet, sour, high, low, large, small; for each day's gift, its mystery, its hope; for the season that surrounds us, blue air, full sun, and laughter running free; for the ministries of healing, the body mended, and the heart made glad; and for thyself, O God, our mercy, pardon, and our peace: we praise thee and cry glory to thy name! Amen.

June — *Second Sunday*

The Gospels attest to Jesus' capacity for grief but not for grievance. He reveals both God's and man's sorrow over "man's inhumanity to man"; but he makes clear that man's initial condition, his mortality, his loss of innocence, his betrayal of love, lie prior to man's problems. It is man's fallen nature out of which problems arise. Grievance is concerned with the problems. Grief focuses on the human nature that brings forth the problems. Grievance leads us to anger, to demanding our rights, to placing the blame on those who are against us, to claiming that righteousness and even God himself are on our side only. Grief goes deeper, is wiser; is, finally and in an eternal sense, more realistic and truer to the facts. For grief has patience, demands no rights, understands guilt is as much a part of the blamer as the blamed, knows that righteousness in a pure sense is only found in God himself. We are resident in an age chaotic and angry with grievances crying out on all sides of us and fermenting wildly within us. And, no doubt, it is necessary that grievances be shouted in the streets, so that the deaf and the indifferent may hear and see and feel. But grievances will never be solved by grievance. A grievance will be transformed and its need met only by those capable of grief, those who know in their flesh the agonies of man and are troubled at heart by the sadness of God.

Almighty God, who orders earth and seasons, stars and men: make lively the cause of our worship. Stand us on holy ground. Keep us in faith. Lift up our eyes on high. And send us forth in love where men cry out, and hearts are broken, and souls demand such mercy as only heaven gives. And so for everyman we pray thyself within his flesh, thy grace teaching him glory, thy peace keeping him sure against all evil days; through Jesus Christ our Lord. Amen.

O God, for all within us that has wounded others and caused them grievance, we ask thy pardon. For the malice in us, and the jealousy, and the cold heart, we pray thy forgiveness. And, above all, we cry thy mercy for our part in the general misery of mankind: for our deaf ears that will not hear and our blind eyes that will not see. Awaken our pity, strengthen our love; through Jesus Christ who came to save and to set free. Amen.

We give thee thanks, most gracious Lord, for this green time and sun, the walks of love, small children, shelter from storm, and the blessings of sleep. We praise thee for all the times and places where men have set compassion before hate and have accepted, for the sake of us all, more than their share of the wounds and the sorrow. We glorify thee that, undergirding all of earth's teeming life, all chaos and calm, all clamor and silence, is thy peace—awesome, amazing, and eternal. Amen.

June — *Third Sunday*

Surely one of the causes of the moral paralysis of our age is the general agreement among most men, including those who find themselves within the church, that truth is relative, that we live not by any great truth but by countless—often conflicting—little truths. To be sure, recognizing that other men have their truth even as we have ours is a humbling fact and can keep us from a variety of dogma that always insists upon having its own way. At the same time, a thoughtful man will realize that, if all truth is relative, then no truth ultimately abides. Morever, if truth be relative, so also is goodness. We can act but never with final conviction; for tomorrow what we did may be looked upon as useless, if not evil. Over against these relativisms that keep us unwilling to act and wary of taking on responsibilities, lest both action and responsibility prove meaningless or wrong, is the Christian Truth which is not an idea but an embodiment, not a value judgment but an incarnation. It is the Truth made flesh. It is the good of God himself, the eternal Truth, lived out in the bone and mind and souls of men.

June — *Third Sunday*

O blessed Trinity, be with us in our worship. Open to us the holy creation going on all around us: the spindrift airs, the green walks, the morning and the evening songs. Let thy Word be in us, lively and full of grace and fraught with healing. And send the Comforter, even the Holy Ghost, to assail our complacencies and awaken us to thy will. Amen.

O God, we who profess and call ourselves Christians confess that we have connived, swaggered, hated, abused, lied—all to our own vainglory. We have been busy with being busy. We have settled down in the soggy status quo. We don't like to be disturbed by the holy mysteries that come tumbling across the hours and the days. We let our souls fall asleep. Forgive us our sins. Keep us in grace. Amen.

Our five and urgent senses praise thee, O God, for large summer sights, sweet airs, sounds within sounds, gifts within gifts. Our hearts praise thee for suffering transformed, for sorrow comforted, for joy extravagantly given. Our minds praise thee for the disciplines of learning, the conversations of wisdom, the parables of truth. Our souls praise thee for thy Love endlessly persuading us out of our darkness into thy marvelous light; through Jesus Christ our Lord. Amen.

June — Fourth Sunday

What is characteristic of most people in our time is that we have learned not to believe in anything or anyone too strongly. True, we are all capable of a brief passion over a political campaign, the tax rate, flagrant injustices, outbreaks of crime. And we give the nod, hardly with awareness that we do so, to an amazing number of attitudes and ideas that were, when originally proposed, dangerous and soul-searching. Probably all of us, at one time or another, had an earnest desire to seek out the truth of things; we wanted to know the true from the false, the right from the wrong, the real from the make-believe. As we grow older, we settle into the comfortable grooves, try to keep out of harm's way, and play most of each day's life by ear. And this safe ritual is just as much a habit in religion as in any other department of our living. We don't want to be pressed, pushed, or involved in too much of anything—particularly in the area of the unsettled and unsettling questions. Because we have avoided the questions with such dexterity, we have little in us that can be shaken and transformed by the great, disturbing answers.

June — Fourth Sunday

Almighty God, you stand giant beyond us and yet walk closely and surely in the human heart. Be present now with all thy people gathered in thy name. Dazzle us. Amaze us. Persuade us. Place high heaven over us and the holy gospel against us and Jesus Christ before us; so that, shaken out of our nonsense, our vanity, and our pride, we will this day adore thee and everyday seek thee and all days trust thee. Amen.

O God, we are tangled up in the usual and ancient knots, the strings and snarls of the world, the flesh, and the devil. We are anxious over many things that do not matter. We love the fats and honeys and cushions for both body and mind. We are wooed, and often won, by the comfortable lie. We gain the whole world and lose our souls. O we are troubled, terrored, torn. Come, gracious One. Cut the sagging web, untie the knots, make taut the guidelines that we may shake free from the softness and walk the land in power; through Jesus Christ our Lord. Amen.

Yea, Lord, we praise thee in the morning congregation and at the noonday under the high sun and in the evening before sleep. For thou art the mystery that breathes our breath, the inventor of daylight, the guardian of death. Thou art the beginning, the race, and the repose. By thy Mercies the fallen never finally fall, nor are the lost truly lost, nor do the dead die. All is well in thee and shall be well forever and ever. Amen.

We have heard it said on some rather impeccable authority that a man should love his neighbor as he loves himself. Most of us like the sound of this saying; and, in a bumbling way, we set out to practice it. In our own neighborhood there has been a pleasant conversation going on for a long time. We do help the injured and care for the lonely; we provide hikes and games and feasts for one another's children; we loan tools and lawn mowers; we hold teas and coffee hours. Like the Samaritan we try to be sensitive to our neighbor's needs; and, as is often said, we do the best we can to meet those needs. Interestingly, to love one's neighbor, a man must love himself. Here is a startling, penetrating prelude to what neighborhood means. By what measure shall a man love himself? The measure has much to do with how much we are willing to risk ourselves in the presence of God, with how much we dare to place our height against God's height. The nature of the love toward self insists that a man, whether he knows it or not, has divine or eternal dimensions. And so does his neighbor.

July First Sunday

O thou who has sustained us through the night watches and brought us in mercy to this new day: awaken us, indwell in us, encompass us. Shake out our drowsy souls for praise. Strengthen our hearts for love. Straighten our minds for truth. And turn us from all pantomimes to see our true life in thee and in a warm care for all the neighborhoods of men. Amen.

O God, mysterious One, you see us as we are, a people both for and against you, a people caring for and yet indifferent to our neighbor's need. We confess our part in the world's rage. We admit our part in man's sorrow. We know well our part in a thousand unnecessary cruelties small and large. For these acts and for the malice in us, we beseech thy forgiveness. Amen.

By love, O God, thou hast set about us the multitude of our days with airs for spaciousness and with earth as a bulwark, with rainbows of birds and the archery of trees, with hills to heighten us and valleys to deepen us, and everywhere the great family of man to be to us father and mother and brother and sister. In pain, thou art our Solace; in grief, our Comforter; in death, our Redeemer. All praise to thee! Amen.

July — Second Sunday

The time is coming; indeed, the time is at hand, when we must strengthen one another; when we must tell our hearts, say how it is with us, declare what we believe and what we do not believe about God, man, and the world we live in. The age sprawls around us—an age huge in its power, undisciplined in its actions, unmotivated in its purposes. It is an age that boasts that it is always on the edge of paradise or disaster. It is an age going its way on supersonic speeds. It is an age of vast loneliness as the earth spins around the sun in a universe that apparently does not care one way or the other for the people who live on Main Street. And all of us are captive to the speed, the chaos, the size, the race toward some blind destiny that may be no destiny at all. It is not to deny either change or progress that we who are the people of the church must learn again to say to each other how it is with our faith; to declare aloud what God has done in us, for us, with us. We must revive our center and take the consequences; that is, we must risk that dangerous and exciting weather of living where faith reveals itself to faith, experience to experience, hope to hope, grace to grace, and love to love.

July — Second Sunday

Come, thou creator, thou immensity of love, thou eternity of mercy. Come, and be with us and in us and beside us and over us. Be as hands upon us, and fashion us for shining. Be as warmth within us, and fire us for caring. Be as strength beside us, and shape our lives for healing. Abide in our prayers, the spoken and unspoken; and make thy Word come true in our flesh; through Jesus Christ our Lord. Amen.

O God, we come before thee contrite and sad and eager to mend our ways. Forgive us for the times we have bullied the little people and for the places we have tried to be first in line; for the times of our anger and the places of our stupidity; for the times of our cowardice and the places of our hesitation; for every time and place we did not love the goodness of men, nor praise the glory of God. Forgive us and heal us this day; through Jesus Christ our Lord. Amen.

We thank thee, gracious Lord, for another day of life; for bread upon our tables; for friends who love us in spite of what we are; for mercy given us beyond our deserving; for the summer sparrow; for the immeasurable joy of joy; for the holy saints and the holy heretics; and for Jesus Christ, our risen Lord, unto whom with thee and the Holy Ghost, be all glory and majesty, dominion and power, world without end. Amen.

July — *Third Sunday*

There are large words hurled and heard across the world today: peace, freedom, understanding, brotherhood. These are words freighted with hope, words that describe how many people in all countries wish the world to be. But merely to say the words is not to make them come true, nor do nations and people mean the same things even though they say the same words. At the level of governments the way to peace and understanding is hard and wearying, and at times almost hopeless. Peace has to be translated into disarmament and signed treaties. Understanding depends upon first learning each other's language and then finding out the meaning behind the languages. Thus, day after day, month by month, the ambassadors and the secretaries and the premiers struggle and agonize over problems and differences not easily resolved. Yet, amazingly and happily, at the level of people our hearts and minds take on greater hope. We have another language that gives meaning to the great words; we have families, music, the daily job, falling in love, laughing at our own mistakes, and just being human beings before we are special nationalities. We carry the real peace of the world in our bodies and in our friendships together.

July — *Third Sunday*

Great God, thou art a mighty strength round about the turning world. Each city and village rests on thy mercy. The air blows and calms at thy bidding. A man arises and goes his way, because thou art God. Delight, spacious and huge delight, is in the man who puts his trust in thee: in birth, in life, in death, and even forever. Amen.

O God, we unburden ourselves before thee, out of a need for a great mercy; for we have sinned and done much evil in thy sight. We have lied to ourselves about ourselves and worn masks and not trusted in love. We have been unfaithful to the goodness in others. We have dealt as misers with hope. We fret over illusions and refuse the realities that give us life. Yea, Lord, we sin, we fail, we fall. Forgive us. Lift us up. Redeem us; through Christ our Lord. Amen.

O God, we praise thee for the small places of peace: the child at play, hands honestly at work, the quiet family, love in the eyes of friends, forgiveness in the words of our enemies, the listening man. We praise thee for all who bring tidings of peace: the singer, the doctor, the teacher, the dreamer; and all who, in trust, build up the waste places and turn the ashes of mourning into a garland of joy. Glory to God in the highest. Amen.

July — Fourth Sunday

At the close of Paul's letter to the Romans, a document heavily saturated with theology and doctrinal concerns, there occurs a chapter of greetings to old friends and fellow workers. Each friend is mentioned by name, and usually a warm word of remembrance is spoken. In another letter Paul has recorded the variety of gifts—personal gifts, that can be used in the service of God. But herein he is satisfied to name people by name, to assert by the very naming that the life of the church is fulfilled in particular persons. It is a refreshing reminder even for us. For a church, though it may well bear the meaning of such great symbols as "the body of Christ," "the new Israel," or "the royal priesthood," is always first a family of people—with names, lives, loves, anxieties, hopes, failures, surprises, deaths. It is so with us today. And yet the church has this peculiarity: it binds people, ordinary everyday people, to each other as they come to know themselves—and each other—as people who are most extraordinary and eternal in the presence of the mysterious and generous and abiding mercy of God.

July — Fourth Sunday

Come unto us, O Lord, and find and enlighten and renew us, one and all. Where we have gone from thee, lead us back in love. Where we live in darkness, take the cloud from our eyes and the heaviness from our souls. Where we wait out our days with fear or hate or boredom, refresh us with such mercy as will turn us again to honor thee in the visible world and to rejoice in thee among the family of man. And put to use whatever gifts we have to build up, to reconcile, and to enjoy; through Jesus Christ our Lord. Amen.

Almighty God, in whose mystery we abide and by whose mercy we are redeemed, we, here and now, confess our sin against mankind and against thee, all our transgressions hidden and open, the evil done and the goodness left undone. We have betrayed the innocents, forgotten the sufferers, and mocked at the peacemakers. Worse, we have denied thee. But for thy forgiveness we are lost, and our brittle world will break, and gladness will know it no more. O save us, gracious Lord. Amen.

Yea, Lord, daily you give us a new world, and colors of air and sun, and expectations to begin again labor, adventure, and adorations. And hourly you are in it all: brooding with love down the morning, arousing the sleepers to your daylight, moving with mercy through the body's ache, bearing the heart's anguish, lifting up the bright resurrections over and over and over. Praise be to your goodness to us and to all men. Amen.

July — *Fifth Sunday*

It is wondrously strange, a thing to marvel at and a fact to sorrow over—the differences we have one from another—those that make life various and alive and those that make life useless and dead. So we rightly rejoice in the variety of gifts and skills men have—even though unequally distributed, it often seems. Praise be for the butcher who is not a baker, for the man of science who does not care for poetry, for blue eyes and red hair and the rainbow of neckties and those who prefer overstuffed chairs to modern furniture—and vice versa. But shame on the angers over color lines, false nationalisms, and the hundred differences that separate us by blindness and pride. We should know better. All mankind should know better and feel deeper and think wiser. See a newborn child; he is the child of everyman. Watch the son grow tall and quick in skills and hope. So everyman's son. There goes a wedding party. Their laughter is ours. Stand by a grave. It is you and I. Under the differences is man, Adam, everyman—frail, lonely, dreaming, failing, dying, rising. Let us pray for all men. They and we are one.

July — *Fifth Sunday*

O God, thou hast delivered us from the dark persuasions of sleep and given us a day, enormous in light, new in hope, and brimming for compassion. Thou hast found us hungry for bread we cannot earn and fed us mercy and toughened our souls with love. Thou hast heard of our fear and felt with us the capture of death and held us in thy might and killed our captor, death. Come, now, to our worship. Amen.

O God, in our generation, who shall save us but yourself, for our other gods have failed us. We have worshiped the image in the little mirrors; we have knelt beside our motorcars; we have prayed to the vitamin tablet, the tranquilizer, and the local bank; we have eaten cake while others went without their bread; and in the name of sweet charity we have given of our surplus change to all worthy causes. O God, in this whirlwind world who can stand except you break a way for him to go, except you light a fire in the world's dark night. Break our idols and turn us home again; through Jesus Christ our Lord. Amen.

Praise to God our Father who made all worlds and this world, and gave man breath and generation, and sent himself in messengers and prophets, and placed against all dark his Radiance, even Jesus Christ our Lord. Praise to God the Son, who made mercy walk and love to dance and death to die. Praise to God the Holy Ghost who sifts and sorts, comforts and gathers, opens and persuades, that everyman shall know the time of his visitation. Praise Father, Son, and Holy Ghost. Amen.

August — First Sunday

Others tell us and we frequently tell ourselves that the church, though it says many wonderful things, is not relevant to the world; that the church talks and talks and talks but doesn't do very much. If this be true (and surely there is much truth in noticing that the church doesn't perform its preaching always very efficiently, very wisely, or very well), it may seem strange to affirm that there is still something more significant than what the church does—a question to be asked, a return to be made, a remembrance to be recaptured which is prior to what we do. This question is a wondering about beginnings, an awe about the origins of life. It is a return to the great depth out of which all action finally must arise if what men do is to have any ultimate meaning. It is a remembrance of what it means to speak the praises of life and the praises of God, of declaring the adorations which put fire and hope and relevance into what we do in God's name.

August — First Sunday

God, we are come with need, hope, dream, anger, fear, weariness. And now we say, this day, somehow, not surely, not always faithfully, using some double-talk, wanting as usual to have our cake and eat it—now we say we want you with us and in us and around us and before us. Help us. Fulfill us. Awaken us. Calm us. Love us. Refresh us. Deep within we know, like we know our hands, that only in you do the days and the nights make sense, come alive, shout joy. Come now, O Father, Son, and Holy Ghost. Amen.

O Lord, how shall we present ourselves before you? We are so often a stiff-necked, contrary people; careful with things, careless with persons; apt in taking, awkward in giving; quick with anger, slow with forgiveness; in love with our fears and in fear of our loves; busy with falsehood, idle with truth. By your imponderable and generous mercy erase our surfaces and deepen us down in the places of your glory; through Jesus Christ our Lord. Amen.

O God, thou towering, thou gentle, thou hidden, thou immediate, receive us by wonder, thanks, awe, joy. We are small; thou art great. We are cruel; thou art kind. We hear thee out beyond the wind's music, beyond the seasons, beyond the vision. We touch thee quick, close at hand, in children, in the marriage song, beside the dying. O receive in us and from us by silence, gesture, sigh, murmur, shout—our praise that all the world resides in thee. Amen.

August — Second Sunday

There are many pictures of the church that we hold in the mind's eye and in the heart's remembering—a white meetinghouse, a climbing spire, an old hymn, a deacon who practiced what was preached, the bustle of a church supper or fair, a child all bonneted and pink for Easter day. These are kind and gentle memories. Who can deny them? But by them alone the church can neither live nor serve. For the church has a present tense and a world around it deeply troubled and confused which requires from the church more than even its best platitudes. What, then, shall we say of these things? When the church is alive, the people in it gather faithfully to cast themselves against the ultimate questions: Who am I? What is man? What is the meaning of my life and my death? Is there a purpose and a reason and a hope in being born? Thus, the church is the questioning community. The church, too, is the listening community. It hurls its questions at the mystery of God and waits upon his answers. And the answer comes that the church's life is to be the redemptive community—the people who minister, bind up, heal—but never perfectly—always as people who themselves need healing.

August — Second Sunday

O God, now is our conversation, silent and spoken, of thyself and in thyself. Thy word is upon our words; thy strength is upon our strengths; thy love is upon our loves. O carry into our prayers a restless and deep cry for those that are sick, for those that are tangled in hates, and for those who are afraid. Especially keep in thy care the innocent, and bear up them that be downcast and brokenhearted. So we pray for all men, and so may all men pray for us; through Jesus Christ our Lord who healeth all our diseases. Amen.

O God, it is in us all: the world's anger, the private grievances, the pride that goes before the fall, the fear that gnaws away our trust. We move in darkness; we are tired with labor that does not satisfy; we are possessed by our possessions. We seek after you aimlessly and listen to you casually. We are confused. Great Lord, clarify our days and nights. Center us down on the first things. Awaken us from our sleep. Prod us and prepare us for the forgiveness for which we dare to ask, and whip us into life with the lash of your joy. Amen.

Say we in our hearts that it is the God who made heaven and earth who guarded us while we slept and awakened us to this new day. And let us rejoice that in him the weak are made strong and the foolish made wise, that by his mercy the broken are mended and the lost ones returned home. Let us always be giving praise, because somewhere and somehow in the world's tangle, he names us and makes us his forever. Amen.

August — Third Sunday

The church has never really been the church except as it stretched beyond itself, except it pointed to something beyond itself. In the building of churches this was always accomplished by a spire or a cupola lofted above the great assembly room where the people gathered and pointing toward heaven like faith's very finger. And within the church as it gathered at worship the hymns ascended, the prayers clamored upward toward God, and the word of God read from the pulpit and faithfully preached was a constant reminder of the high and holy mystery of God who created heaven and earth.

But even as the spire soared and the prayers reached and the preached word announced the glory of God, so there returned earthward the gifts of God to each man in the gathered congregation, so came back an alleluia to respond to the sacred songs of the people, so returned in amazing miracle answers to men's prayers, and so was given out of the divine mystery a way of life to be lived when formal worship paused and men returned to their homes, their work, and their world.

It is so even to this day.

August *Third Sunday*

O God, we place before thee such prayers out of our silence as shake the hearts of all men everywhere. We cry peace, when there is no peace. We beseech thee for the hungry who are not fed, the naked who are not clothed, the prisoners who are not set free. We ask for justice where we have refused it. Though the words come hard, we pray that our enemies, personal and political, receive overwhelmingly thy love, thy care. Find in our prayers something more than the hypocrisies that hem them in. Amen.

O God, in your plenteous mercy, receive our confession, for we have accepted your goodness and given you no thanks; we have fought against the disciplines of your love; we have playacted in worship and sought to bribe you with our prayers; we have been afraid of your presence and hidden from you in a thousand devious ways; we have run from your salvation. Pity us, pity us, O God; and hold us patiently, until in our hearts we know that we are yours forever. Amen.

O God, your mystery is the light beyond our dark. You redeem us from dread and evil. You awaken us to morning, and in the night you gather us to rest. You are unknown yet known, distant but close, beginning yet end. We see your beauty and are amazed; we receive your strength and have new hope; we are held in your mercy and are at peace. Now we declare our joy in you. Amen.

August *Fourth Sunday*

There is a kind of cold common sense that we ought to apply to the life of the church—a common sense that we are not reluctant to apply in most other areas of our living. Perhaps, it is more than common sense. It is a shrewdness that asks of what we do: "Of what use is it?" It is a canny wisdom that asks of what we possess: "Of what use is it?" So we are both practical and wise when we ask of what we do and what we possess in the church: "Of what use is it?" Yet, asking this question, we discover a prior question; namely, "What is the life of the church for? What is its purpose?" Apparently the life of the church as the twentieth century knows it to be is a fairly accurate facsimile of the society which surrounds it—busy, prosperous, and utterly confused. True, we have a nodding acquaintance with the ancient metaphors of the church as "the city of God, the city that hath foundations," as the center of man's salvation. Ironically, in a time when what men need most is, indeed, to be saved, we no longer understand what salvation means to us or requires of us. When we begin to hear again the vast implications of salvation, we will find anew the reason for the church and will know what is of use—and what, indeed, is of no use.

August — Fourth Sunday

O God, you return us to the morning and the new day's promises. As the night has fled and the darkness gone from us by your mighty will, so in you may the evil hour be prevented and our sins be removed far from us. Provide us with strength to work our work well and gladly. Keep us faithful to all rituals of service and compassion; and, in all that we are and think and do, lead us forever to the thresholds of praise; through Jesus Christ our Lord. Amen.

Gracious God, who hath called us into thy church, the community of grace, the household of faith: we confess that we have been indifferent and unprofitable servants. Called to practices of love, we have been neither hot nor cold; called to celebrations of mercy, we have neither sacrificed nor suffered. We follow the safe path, the respectable street, the approved highway—lest we encounter thy mystery, thy danger, and thy cross. O Lord, save us from the misery of the neutral way, and strengthen us to lose ourselves in the wilderness of the world's anguish. Help us to go without fear; and make us one with the patriarchs, prophets, apostles, martyrs, saints—a true church of redemption; through Jesus Christ our Lord. Amen.

You give grace, great Lord: delight that quickens the doldrum mind, solace that sings in grief, peace that sweetens the dry cup of hate. You give hope, good Lord: strength to the broken bones, laughter before the solemn mirrors, caress in the time of loneliness. You give truth, wise Lord: love thrust against fear, forgiveness wedged against sin, trust shaped against death. You give us grace, hope, and truth, and blessed is your name. Amen.

September — First Sunday

I find myself daily and passionately persuaded to the presence of God in all things and persuaded equally that every man is born to be blessed, to accept joy—if not in his own time, in God's time. To say this is not in any way to minimize the agonies of our age or to deny the evil, apparently unmerited, that overtakes us, or to make light of the peril that now so manifestly surrounds us. On the contrary, it is to affirm that the blessed man is he who moves flesh and bone, mind and heart, most fully into the suffering and the bewilderment of his world. The paradox of joy in Christian experience is truly that "he who would save his life must lose it." The environment of blessedness as declared in the Beatitudes is poverty in spirit, mourning, meekness, persecution for the sake of righteousness and God. We exalt pride in spirit, hide from death, deplore humility, avoid suffering, substitute manners for righteousness, and make God an idea for discussion. Yet the signs of his presence are all around us, and his joy is endlessly given to each of us not taken in by the facades of fear and the cleverness of cynics.

September — First Sunday

O God, out of gladness we praise thee for this day and its countless new occasions. Help us to walk its crisp weather with strong strides of faith. Turn the routines of work into the ceremonies of joy, and teach us to become minstrels of thy glory. Amen.

O sovereign Lord, because thy mercies, tender and passionate, everywhere surround us, we tremble and sorrow in our sins; for we know well the times of our negligence, our bad beginnings and our poor endings. How little we desire to serve thee and praise thee. We have good words and lazy deeds, and we turn thy magnificent love from us and play with the jackstraws of our own foolishness. O God, take this little repentance and make it great. Amen.

O God, for the everyday morning by which we can begin again, for the body's wakefulness to love, for the mind's return to possibility, for the heart's recall to eurekas of hope, and for the soul's new gaze at thyself and thy world, we praise thee this day and declare our lives are for thee forever and ever. Amen.

"But if the salt hath lost its savor . . ."

We should not read these words lightly. They are a parable for our own time as well as for any other. They simply tell the truth; they state the facts, namely: that when men lose their souls, when the savor has gone out of them, they are good for nothing and are cast out and trodden underfoot—in one way or another. And when one man falls, when one man loses his meaning, when one man is denied his fullness, when in one man's eyes the shining of hope dies out, every other man is diminished thereby. Where there is human waste, human loss, human dying, all are wasted, all lose, all die.

Let us be troubled by this. Let our waking and our sleeping be disturbed. Let us be hurt by the hard cruelty that sometimes we can do little or nothing to give back life, to find the lost, to redeem the waste places. It will chasten us. It will clarify lucidly and in large letters why Jesus Christ had to die upon the cross.

O Lord, be with us so that we feel thee like hands upon us; uphold us so that we know thee like strength beneath us; go with us so that we have thee like love within us. Be for us in our goodness and against us in our evil. Keep us from all things shallow and unholy, and move our wills to seek the deep being of thyself. Protect us from all times and places that destroy and deceive, and give us grace to show the justice and mercy to all men that we would ask for ourselves. Make fruitful our prayers; through Jesus Christ our Lord. Amen.

Gracious God, our sins are many. Some we can see and some we cannot see and some we do not want to see. Each of us has his own sin, and yet we share in all men's sins. Whether we go up or down or to right or left, these sins besiege us and prison us. They are heavy and cripple us for running free. They deaden us down even before death. O Lord, we need help to make us whole again. Amen.

Unto God be all praise this day for our deliverance from our separate darknesses; for all within us that kneels; for the penitence in our hearts; for the holy gospel's tidings of our peace; and for Jesus Christ, the lowly One, who for our sakes wore the rags of suffering and sin, and with love's net captures and holds back death for our salvation. All praise to Father, Son, and Holy Ghost. Amen.

September — Third Sunday

"Blessed are the pure in heart, for they shall see God."

The terror of our times is its clutter, its burden of nonessentials, its mounds of nothings that heavy-weight our households and our hearts. And every day we go forth to labor for the bread that does not satisfy; and yet so strong is the habit, so effective the propagandas of our successful "betters," that we return to our homes assured that the crumbs we have gathered up are really cake. Oh, the pity that Christians are willing contributors to this tangle, this false busyness, this unhappy confusion of means and ends.

There is a chastity of being, a nakedness of spirit a man needs, to live with sanity, with height, with hope, with fulfillment. "Blessed are the pure in heart," those with the single eye, those who seek the Holy Grail, those who seek always the "city which hath foundations." To move through the clutter, to throw off the nonessentials like a pedlar his pack, to refuse the nothings—this is "blessedness"; herein we see God.

September — Third Sunday

Vast God, come to us who dare to come before thee. Visit us in thy mystery, moving upon us and against us and through us thy hiddenness and thy clamorous glory that no prayers can tongue and no words hold. Overturn us in our self-assurance. Show us how sanitary, sleek, and dull we are who cry Lord, Lord. Make us utterly weary of the clichés we recite to one another in thy name. Awaken us to holiness and awe that we may approach thee on our very doorsteps; through Jesus Christ our Lord. Amen.

O God, attend our confession. Sin sits in us like a spider spinning a dark web, tightening our fears, binding the wings of hope, drying out love, eating us empty and dead. Sin has a venom and strikes as a death. Sin stuns, stupefies, cripples. Come, celestial One, with the broom of thy grace and sweep away the tangle, the evil, and the dark. Be antidote that in thy power we may be whole again; through Jesus Christ our Lord. Amen.

It is God who sustains us when we rise in the morning and go forth to our work; it is his hand that holds us, his enormous hand that holds us so that we cannot fall, his enormous love that surrounds and upholds us like a battalion of guardian angels. It is God and it is his hand and it is his love that rise with us in the morning and go with us to our work and keep us from falling forever and ever—and ever. Praise ye the Lord. Amen.

September — Fourth Sunday

"Blessed are those that mourn for they shall be comforted."

Grief comes to us in ways that we do not expect; and the heart is troubled, and the soul has its anguish. We rightly understand that Christian faith has a solace for grief, for all the human sadness that ever was, for private sorrow and for public pain. But in order to receive the solace we have some learning to do about the mysteries of grief and the practices of faith. For, often, when we ask what comfort there is for the troubled heart and soul, we are seeking magic, some easy and quick answer, some formula to make everything hard and bad all right again. But we cannot have the comfort of God if we have paid no attention to God. We cannot know the solace of love—even human love—if we have not loved. Moreover, we tend to deny that being troubled in heart and soul can have a meaning. It seems so frequently the blank wall, the hopeless end of all that matters. And yet grief is a gateway to life. It is a central way to all that does matter. By it a man is led to distinguish between the life that endures and the life that passes away. By our participation in the anguish of the world we learn that we belong to the human race. We learn how much we need each other. We find our eternity. This is why Jesus could say: "Blessed are those that mourn. They shall be comforted."

O God, give us the patience in the silence of minutes to wait upon thy timelessness. Deepen us down to listen for thy coming among us. Give us honesty before our own needs and give us compassion before the needs of others. Wound us with the war, the ghettos, the famines of body and soul for all the world's children, the lonely and sick people near us, the burdens of the young. Hear our prayers. Amen.

O sovereign Lord, there is no mending of our sins save by your mercy. We are as purposeless as grasshoppers; and, in the midst of the whirl and rush and fastness of our lives, we have few silences to hear your voice, small place for your presence, and little time for your truths. Our way is tangled; our boasts are foolish; our truths are soiled. O awesome Majesty, gather us and hold us, lest we perish in the holocaust of pride. Amen.

Almighty God, now are our hearts made glad and our tongues like the singing of birds and our bodies like fires, because our trust is in thee: that in thee, this day will be held in strength and given in mercy; that in thee, despite the forests of pain, the ways of laughter shall be found; that in thee, though perils shall surround us, the victory will go to love; that in thee a man can rejoice now and tomorrow and on the day of his dying. Blessed be thy holy name forever and ever. Amen.

October *First Sunday*

Most men in our present age catch a glimpse of what "time" means: that earth, for example, began millions of years ago and that the origin of the universe is cast farther back in the mystery of time than we have zeros to reckon with. Space is equally with us. Yet space now is the new ocean that leads only on and on and on. We falter for language to explain it, except that space is sizable enough to house galaxies and stars more in number than the sands. Strangely, it is even more difficult for men to grasp the significance of human history with all that it reveals to us of the rise and fall of civilizations, with all that it teaches us about ourselves but from which we rarely learn. "Everything changes," declared an ancient sage. "The nations are as a drop in the bucket," cries Isaiah. And finally man—each individual man—comes face-to-face with his own personal history: his birth, his life, his death. And of each of us the psalmist declares: "Our days are like grass. . . . We spend our years as a tale that is told." Yet our days are also full of sounding joy, delight beyond our understanding. What does our private history mean in the presence of mankind's history, against time and space?

October — First Sunday

O thou Hidden-yet-seen, thou Always-yet-now, thou Spirit-yet-flesh, come upon us as sight to our darkness, as act to our waiting, as body to our dreaming. Teach us again and again thy mystery from which we come and to which we will return. Stand thine eternity in our streets, among the people and the governors, beside our missiles and our monuments. Be as a fire to warm us into love, and such a burning as makes us to give light. Be seen now in our flesh; through Christ our Lord. Amen.

O Majesty, behold in pity what we are. Turn aside from thy mountains and thy stars and have mercy upon us. For we dwell in sin. We are proud in the imagination of our hearts. We make wars. We send the hungry empty away. We are lazy before thy truth, and casual and crude in the holy places. We have sought our own safety, denied justice, overlooked falsehood, applauded greed. We have sown the wind and reaped the whirlwind. Come to us, good Lord. Defend us from ourselves; and by thine enormous forgiveness, restore in us a right mind, a faithful heart, and a rejoicing soul; through Jesus Christ our Lord. Amen.

Now in this season of mists and mellow fruitfulness, when apples redden and leaves yellow on the bough; in this time of schoolchildren, when laughter rings on the streets; in this open air of harvests and homecomings, of the day's labor and the night's rest; we praise our God who blesses us in every breath and keeps us in his care morning and evening, over and over, forever and ever. Amen.

October — Second Sunday

I think, often, looking at the autumn, how this time of year captures so well the paradox of being man. It has fire and rigor and tastes out of heaven itself. Yet it is a dying away, a lostness, an ending. And there are many thoughts running against the dazzle in a world heaping up its injustices and its angers all around us, in a world wild with questions that have no easy answers. I find myself, simply as man, as ablaze with hope and delight as any burning bush; but even as I look, I carry in my middle-class body the shame of Oxford, Mississippi, and the shame of blows as old as Hiroshima. It comes over me that the truth is that we are either hopeful people without hope or hopeless people with such hope as we have never dreamed. We live in this tension. Simply as man, no one of us can resolve it. But as Christian man, we cannot only resolve the anguish and the meaningless terror, we can live in the midst of it, handle it, be stricken by it—because we know that it is the luminous tree, the living God that endures with an endurance glorious and joyful.

October — Second Sunday

Blessed Lord, we bring what we are to adore thee: the hands tired after the harvest is in, the gay sights our eyes have seen and their remembrances of sorrow, the mind in us running wisely or foolishly the broken field of each day, and the heart's enormous loves. Find us in our praise, O God, for beyond our high words and handsome songs it is ourselves we give back. Take us and use us to thy glory; through Jesus Christ our Lord. Amen.

O God, before your awesome righteousness, who can stand? You are holy; we are soiled. You are wholeness; we are brokenness. You are free; we are captive. We have done evil; but worse, we have let evil be done. We have let innocence be attacked; we, too, have fed the dogs of hate. We have watched the world fall. O vast and merciful God, hear our sorrow for what we are when we forget you in your majesty and man in his dignity. Forgive us our sins; through Jesus Christ our Lord. Amen.

Now on this new day, let us praise God who over the cities of darkness sends light and into the valleys the winds and the colors of each season. Let us praise God. He is outside our ships that sail on ocean or in space. It is he who keeps the stars and commands the lightning even to this day. Let us praise God. He gives us the first breath and the last, the bones for walking and the bones for lying down. He only knows the secrets of our hearts, and he alone can redeem us. Let us praise God forever and ever. Amen.

October — Third Sunday

Man, who goes forth to his work in the morning—to desk or field, to lathe or classroom—moves, though he moves faster by motorcar or plane, the ancient path after his daily bread and plods or runs, as all men must, the road to his own dying. He moves in space, yet even more in time. Being born out of mystery he marches by his own strength only as far as the gate marked "death." He comes to a season, "That time of year when yellow leaves or few or none do hang upon the boughs"; he reads in woods and pasture the truth about himself and all men: in the morning they are like grass which "groweth up; in the evening it is cut down, and withereth." To meditate thus is to come of age, for only the mature can stand at the edge of his life and behold his pilgrimage. For wisdom dwells in us when in the midst of the thousand events that occupy us we see ourselves as we really are. Indeed, it is in contemplating the autumn of our living that we become ready to receive in its rich, redounding, resonant glory the Truth more wonderful than the truth about ourselves—the Truth which is God's Truth—the Love that will not let us go.

October — Third Sunday

O God, the airs encompass us. We live, and stand once more in holy church among thy mysteries. Now is our conversation, silent and spoken, of thyself; and thy word is upon our words, and thy strength upon our strengths, and thy love upon our loves. All is mountainous and high; all is valley and deep. We dwell in safety who dwell in thee, and all is a praise. Amen.

Almighty God, what can we say to thee? We are as we are: sometimes plump and self-satisfied, having no need of thee; sometimes crippled and torn, having no love for thee; sometimes empty and afraid, having no trust in thee. We are as we are: never having sought thee seriously, never having listened to thee earnestly, never having followed thee faithfully. We are as we are. Enter us, O God. Astonish us. Overcome us. Heaven in us this day and even forevermore. Amen.

For this day's gift, its mystery, and its hope, we praise thee, O God. For the season that surrounds us, the gray air, the leaning sun, leaves spilled, and laughter, we praise thee, O God. For the ministries of healing, the body mended, the heart made glad, and the mind set free, we praise thee, O God. For thyself, whom we see in Jesus Christ, our mercy, our pardon, and our peace, we praise thee, O God, forever and ever. Amen.

October — Reformation Sunday

The Protestant Reformation produced a certain kind of man, one who when he received the gifts of the Reformation used them and became responsible for them. Being "justified by faith," he devoted his life to the practices of faith. Given the "open Bible" in his own tongue, he read scripture so that it became part of his speech, his bone, and his blood. Understanding anew that "every man is a priest," he became personally involved in a ministry to other men. On his job—butcher, baker, or candlestick-maker—he wrought his task to the glory of God. And he knew in his heart that the highest calling of a man is to be the servant of the Lord Jesus Christ. In a fundamental way the Reformation man was a man reawakened to the forgiveness of God, open like radar to the sovereign mystery of God, and certain that the central purpose of the church is to be a redemptive community, a hospital for the sick, a home for the lost, and a setting-forth place for those courageous and eager to bear the good tidings of great joy which shall be to all people.

Measure yourself against this man. Do we take his name in vain? If he unlocked us from the bondage of medievalism—does our freedom really include his responsibility?

Reformation Sunday

Almighty God, fall upon us like the whirlwind and blow against our sins and drive far from us the evil and temptations. Lift up our eyes to see thee where we are. Put heaven in the work of our hands, and help our days to arise in thy praise and return to thy mercy. Make us a glad people bound in thy love, readied by thy strength, and faithful in thy service; through Jesus Christ our Lord. Amen.

O God, we are towered over by all that we do not understand; we are hemmed in by the world's evil; we are lost in the tangle of our own sins. We avert our eyes from the terror. We turn our back on the wounds. We want to keep what we have. We want a little justice for mankind but not enough to disturb us. We are fat, comfortable, and afraid. Unto thee we confess and cry mercy. Love us in spite of ourselves and forgive us beyond our deserving. And give us again such trust in thee that we shall dare again to fight the dragons of darkness, heal the wounds, require justice, and hold fast to the practices of compassion; through Jesus Christ our Lord. Amen.

O God, for those bold men charred by the fire of heaven to bring us light; for Isaiah and Amos crying havoc to idolatry and injustice; for Paul, weighted down by human dark, and yet alive with grace for all mankind; for Francis, God's poor man, heretic, and saint; for Luther wrestling his wild beasts for our faith; for Calvin speaking thy radiance, thy mystery, and thy power; for these and every man who wills thy will be done, thy love be loved, we praise thy holy name. Amen.

November — First Sunday

Part of the sickness of our time, our human condition, is surely caught upon the word distrust, that way of dealing with life always with the suspicious eye and the doubting heart. The companion of distrust is "fear," and—alas!—as it is written, "Fear hath a torment"; and torment is often upon us, marked on our foreheads, twisted into the habit of our being.

God desires more for man than this. Against distrust, he bulwarks faith; against fear he raises love; against torment he casts up peace. Truly he desires his people, the church, to use these strengthening gifts of which he himself is the guarantee. It is time to draw the little islands we live within into the root and structure of the mainland; it is time to unmask and tell our hearts one to another; it is time to deepen down into our true reason for being—to be the people of the resurrection, daily testifying to this by our trust of ourselves, of other people and the world, and of the very God by whose bounty and breath and redemptive power we and all men live.

November

First Sunday

O Majestic, O Compassionate, O most Holy, we gather to thy praise, and pray that we may be worthy, and that we may be ready, and that we may receive thee. Let fall upon us such forgiveness as shames us from our sin. Shape in our bodies the very ache of faith. And brim our hearts to the wild reaches of joy. Place against us now and always thy Mystery to teach us awe. Yet, in the moment of each breath, be close and gather us in love; through Jesus Christ our Lord. Amen.

O God, we confess that we have treated life shabbily, that we have used people as things, that we have been afraid to love, that we have closed our eyes to injustice and our hearts to mercy. We have hugged our own piety and kept the church away from the suffering of the world. Give us courage to renounce the comfortable lies by which we live and strengthen us to bear in our time the weight of the world's anguish; through Jesus Christ our Lord. Amen.

God comes! Praise him! He is here! Declare him! Say to the frightened nations, God holds you; and to the lost peoples, he has found you! Cry to the sleek suburbs, he is walking your streets; and to the fat cities, he stampedes in your markets. Hear him. He is the air of hope where the mind dreams and the whirlwind of faith where the heart loves. He comes! He is here! Praise him. Amen.

November — Second Sunday

Here now on this day, in this place, is the holy catholic church. Here are a gathered people, who once were no people and now, after their fashion and according to their faith, are God's people. Here are our selves, our souls and bodies, desirous of making a reasonable sacrifice of praise unto the Lord, though with halting speech and doubtful hearts often making a most unreasonable sacrifice. Here from the farm, the classroom, the office, the household, we come out of habit, duty, hope, joy—who knows why?—to enter a dialogue with the Eternal One, to engage him with questions rooted in the very marrow of our being and let fall upon us the weight and fullness and density of the divine answers. Here we come to gaze upon our own mystery in the presence of God's mystery. Here, unblessed, we come to receive the blessing, though like Jacob of old, having wrestled with the angel or with God himself, we may well be wounded and go limping away—yet learning that grace enters the soul by a wound. And, if we cannot always find here the burning bush, the holy flame—God will yet make a bonfire of the smallest matchsticks of our faith.

November — Second Sunday

O God, thou who art morning and mercy to all our darkness and to all our sorrow, come to us now and make our hearts ready for thy worship. Accept our silences as well as our words, our intentions as well as our actions, our doubts as well as our faith. Mend us where we are broken, enliven us where we are dull, encourage us where we are afraid; and send us out into the world to mend, enliven, and encourage, in the name of the Father, the Son, and the Holy Ghost. Amen.

O God, we pray out of our mystery into thy mystery; a people we are in shadow, and we cry out of our evil unto thy mercy. Sin is our lot. By dark choices of lust we burn; and by envy we smolder. Fear blackens in our bones, and we put our trust in armadas and missiles and the pride of men. We make our worship a cushion and a fine car, and our children mimic us. But in us is an old fire and an ancient vision; our hearts long for the holy places, and our souls wait for the winds of grace. Save us. Amen.

Daily our Lord doth compass with his love all cities, mountains, fields, the rivers of water, all gathering places, and all lonely vigils. He strides among stars and carries the oceans of the air. He sets men free among many wonders. He unrolls each day's adventure as a scroll. Yea, he hears our loneliness and runs to our anguish and dies in our dying. He keeps us from falling and captures us firm in his grace forever and ever. Praise him. Amen.

November — Third Sunday

God demands of us such a little thing that he may give us himself: the lifting of the latch of the mind, the opening of the gate of the heart. For where there is the smallest space that we allow him, he presses in, bringing the gift of his fire to warm our coldness, the gift of his mystery to awaken our dullness, the gift of his mercy to forgive our sin. And yet, before the opening of the door, we have a preparation to go through, a maturing to achieve. This preparing, this maturing, we call the search for God. It can take us into deep, bewildering, and unknown ways. It is a search that cannot be carried on either by superficial faith, by ritual observance, or by acceptance of dogma. It is in essence the honoring of God in one's own experience. Its amazing end is that the God for whom we search has already and always found us even as we sought him.

Almighty God, who beholdeth the nations of the earth as a very little thing yet in whose mercy not one man born is ever lost, be over us as a morning of joy, and beside us as a daylight of power, and within us as an evening of peace. Be companion of our labors, overcomer of our sorrows, and guardian of our lives. Kneel us before every gentleness of life; and keep us unafraid, that in all the weathers of the world, we may go with patience and forbearance, and, in thy name, build up the waste places and set the captives free; through Christ our Lord. Amen.

O God, thou dark, thou light, thou now, thou endless one, hear our prayer, our confession, our sorrow. There is a rage in us against ourselves, against mankind, against thee. There is a sickness in us, an ancient loneliness, an evil in the bone and in the soul. Forgive us for what we are, for what we have done, for what we have not done, for what we will do again. And in thine immeasurable mercy be in us a center of compassion that, day by day, restores us to wholeness, to trust, and to an honest peace with thee, with other people, and within ourselves; through Jesus Christ our Lord. Amen.

O God, we praise thee and thank thee for thyself who takes an acorn and makes it a tree; sets air over us and daylight and the large pictures of each season; gives us the walk and run of the body, the mind's radar, and heart's insatiable dreams. We praise thee and thank thee for thyself who gives us the gifts we do not earn and the strength we do not have and the forgiveness we do not deserve. Unto thee be all glory and honor, dominion and power, world without end. Amen.

November — *Fourth Sunday*

Winter sends us that sufficiency of dark outside us that seems but to make heavier the darkness we carry within us. As the earth turns us from our summertime, there is more dark; and all that we sense of mankind's sorrow and fears magnifies in the long drear weather that surrounds and permeates us on certain sober days. The causes of human kind take on a melancholia. We are led to ponder and wonder on birth and life and dying and death to the point of unrelieved loneliness. And the houses of men and the cities of men remind us mostly of our frailty. We are not finally in command. We build the house, and it shall fall away. We stand the watch guarding all the peoples, protecting as best we can the hearts we love. But though we had invented paradise and secured ourselves against all poverty, all sicknesses, all seasonal colds and darknesses, we are not wise enough or good enough or strong enough. We have the vision of angels and the reach of mortal men at best. How direct is the psalmist: "Except the Lord keep the city, the watchman waketh but in vain."

November — Fourth Sunday

O gracious Lord, we arise to the winter day kept by thy mercy and blest with new hope. Go with us as companion and morning in the drear cold and in all dark hours. Come among us so that our prayers tell the truth of our hearts; and remind us, caught in the aches and fears and dying of the body, of the trust that overcomes pain, the love that casts out fear, and the faith that conquers death. Through Jesus Christ our Lord. Amen.

O God, we have gone from thee hastening down the easy ways of our prosperity, hurrying after shadows, hiding in the lonely crowd. We have prayed to thee—not to disturb us; we would like to meet thee—but not today; we hope we may see thee—at a respectable distance. We would like to take thee seriously—but at some other time. This is our sin, our illness, our lostness. O thou who didst come to forgive sinners, to heal the sick, to find the lost: forgive, heal, and find us; through Jesus Christ our Lord. Amen.

Yea, Lord, we gather to thy glory. We walk, and thou art the power in the blood and the bone and the muscle. We shape and build machineries for earth and air, cities and towers and gorgeous palaces; for thou hast given us hands for instruments and made the mind a dreaming and desiring place. We sing, because thou hast tongued and belled us to be minstrels and dancing men. We love, because for love thou made us most. O Lord, we gather to thy glory. And if thou hast made us mortal men, so in thee shall our mortality put on immortality; through Jesus Christ our Lord. Amen.

November — Thanksgiving Day

Among Christians the one reason for thanksgiving is God himself. It cannot be otherwise, if we in any way understand our human situation: what frail and foolish, though often beloved, creatures we are; how we muddle after happiness; how we waste our substance following shadows; how in the midst of plenty we are spiritually poor; how on the good green earth of God's providing we go about as joyless and hollow men. True, within the church we can "count our blessings" and "go over the river and through the woods" with the sentimentalists; and we can nod our heads respectfully at the Pilgrim Fathers sharing wild turkey with the Indians, and enjoy kodakchrome slides of red barns, silos, stacked corn, and pumpkins against the purple hills. Yet our thanksgiving can arise out of an assurance deeper than our human uncertainty, out of a blessing more eternal than the feast by which we celebrate, out of a power more majestic than New England Indian summer: namely, that it is God who gives us this land, it is God who provides us this feast, and it is God who saves us from ourselves for himself. Thanks be to God!

November — Thanksgiving Day

O thou by whose mystery fields bring forth and by whose purposes the earth turns to its sun and by whose mercies men dare to rise to the new day, incline to our prayers and by thy grace inform them so that what we do and think and say praises and pleases thy majesty. Flood the drought in us. Shake our drowsy spirits. Fashion us for the uses of love. And at every hour, defend us from the sins, small and great, that dry our minds, deaden our hearts, and kill our souls. Keep us always close to thyself; through Jesus Christ our Lord. Amen.

Almighty God, daily we sin and daily we repent. We are demon yet angel, violence yet peace, fear yet love, lust yet chastity, blindness yet sight, blasphemy yet reverence. We despoil, deface, despise, yet we repair, renew, adore. We suffer in the guilt of our guilt, and cry thy mercy, and beseech thy grace in us and upon us that we may be set free within thy forgiveness to honor thee in the kitchen places, on the highroads, and before all men; through Jesus Christ our Lord. Amen.

Yea, thou Lord of us all; thou Sovereign of the air's ocean, the valley's running, the cumbersome mountains; thou Goodness in the taste of our souls: we praise thee for the clamorous and holy seasons; for the furrow, the stalk, the leaf, and the grain; and for the feast all gold and red and high. We praise thee for great mercy toward our sins, for constant love when we are in despair, for strength to rise again in the dark hour. We praise thee for thy peace against our wars, and for thy ways of peace that shall redeem nations. Amen.

November *Fifth Sunday*

The word of comfort comes. Is there a man who does not need it in this day, caught up as we are in hours of human wrath, of wars unsought, of poverties of body at the edges of our suburbs, of poverties of soul in our own living rooms, of children driven by our fears to mockeries of learnings, of ourselves driven by God-knows-what illusions to burn ourselves out trying to be what we are not and were never intended to be? Comfort ye, my people. Oh, to be comforted when we lie awake wondering what sorry compromises we have given assent to, for what a mess of pottage we sold our lives. If a man is fortunate enough to have this ache for comfort! To be torn by the need to have hands, heart, glory, God—somehow moving against, then upon, one's life—as a holiness to give us wholeness, as a gentleness against the angers we think we thrive upon, as a great and spacious laughter to trim down the pomposities by which we so often assume we are succeeding. How much the comfort of God comes, first, like the little boy in "The Emperor's New Clothes" saying—even as Christ in the manger—so much of what we give our time to is pure fraud; and then, second, like the very God at the creation saying so much of what we are intended to be is pure good, pure truth! And this is the double comfort—God as the child and God as the incarnate redeemer. Comfort ye, my people.

November — Fifth Sunday

In the morning our hearts praise you, O God; and in the evening we come before you with thanksgiving. The hours run by in anxious haste, in teeming busyness, in mingled failure and fulfillment. Yet in every second you touch us by your love. You dense us in and dazzle us by your joy. Come to us now. Seize our hands. Brush against our skin. Sun-burst in our hearts. So shall we know you. So shall we be blessed. Amen.

Now, Lord, hear our confession and receive our sorrow for our dullness, our stupidity, our fraud. Yea, seeing you, all love, our sin is a heaviness upon us and in us. We are a very winter of gray and cold. We live half seeing, half hearing, half knowing, half believing. Pity us. Awaken us. Save us. Be archangel in us till we dare to soar; and in all the plodding times and places in the months ahead, be to us unicorn and dove and storm and star, until our flesh becomes your wild, wild Word. Amen.

The gift of the day, great Lord, is the gift of our life, is the gift of your love. You birth us by hillsides of daylight. You breathe in us and bubble power to the blood and kindle joy in the heart. You give us daily an advent of mercies. You send us leaping, somersaulting, capering toward Bethlehem and your good Son. Joy. Joy. Joy. Amen.

Sacraments

The Lord's Supper

December

The Lord's Supper is ritual from its beginning. Over and over the bread is blessed and broken and shared; over and over the cup is blessed and poured and given. It is a feast where God himself is host; it is a ceremony of mercy where in the common stuff men eat and drink God assures and reassures us of his endless faithfulness to us and to all mankind. In this meal God inserts, incarnates, places his eternal love in the most common of human occasions—the bread and cup we eat and drink; and thereby he reminds us that he is always present in our lives, hour by hour, day by day, week by week, year by year. The Lord's Supper is ritual in which God declares *by an action,* over and over, that he gives us love which casts out fear, peace that is beyond our understanding, life that saves us from death.

God is faithful in this rite. It remains for us to come to his table faithfully, to come honestly out of our deepest needs, to come with our sin for forgiveness, to come with our goodness to give praise. We must come desiring nothing less than God himself, desiring, indeed, that our piecemeal life be fed and nourished by the eternal grace that makes us whole again.

The Lord's Supper

December

O thou toward whose majesty the night stars rise and men's eyes and hearts lift up; thou who hast set us in this day with its myriad hopes and its thousand mysteries; thou who dost surround and hold in mercy all that is broken, sinful, and unloved; thou Giver, Gatherer, and Savior; make the hands prayerful that dare to take thy bread; and the tongues that drink thy love, let them speak thy praise. And go with us into the winter darkness that we may fear no evil, that we may take heart upon the loneliest journey; through Jesus Christ our Lord. Amen.

O thou holy One, thou Word made flesh, thou Eternity captived in time, thou Heaven in a manger, thou Light larked down into our darkness, we pray that thou wilt forgive us our sins and make us clean and fair for thy coming. Loose us from our treacheries toward thee and our cruelties toward one another. O so feast us this day on the bread that does not perish that we may arise to new daylights of hope, and give into our hands thy healing Cup whereby we shall be made whole again; through Jesus Christ our Lord. Amen.

Let us be glad in this bread out of the dark earth and in wine of the grape out of the light—that in bread and wine Jesus Christ gives us a true pledge of solace for our pain, forgiveness for our sins, and the very joy that we shall rise at our death in the presence of angels and before our God, the almighty and holy One, who made heaven and earth. Let us be glad and heartily rejoice and praise him forever and ever. Amen.

The Lord's Supper — Christmas Eve

God, whom no one has ever seen, comes to us to be seen in Jesus Christ. He comes to us not as a stone or a tree or a mighty storm (though, in an elementary sense, he has always shown us himself in nature). Rather he enters man's world as a man, thus revealing that the divine nature not only encompasses things but also persons. So in Advent, for us a seasonal time of darkness, we are making ready for the coming of the God who declares himself in Light—but noticeably as Light in the flesh, in a man. Thus, it is amazingly right that we should celebrate the Lord's Supper as we make our preparations for his coming. Indeed, we engage in a marvelous paradox; for, just as God comes to us in flesh, in the body of Christ, so we return to him by means of the flesh, the bread and the wine. Every time we gather for the feast of eucharist (thanksgiving), we engage God with the same reality that he engages us—we partake of the meal that bears Light into darkness, heaven into earth.

Lord of this feast, gather us to the bread that is broken for us and all mankind and to the drink by which we thirst no more; that in thy mercy given, we may arise to new and vigorous days; that in thy promises, we may go without fear in the dark passages; that in thy praise, we may find out why we live. Let thy flesh be our flesh; thy spirit, our spirit; thy power, our power; for thy Self being in us, we will live for love's sake always; through Christ our Lord. Amen.

O Lord, at this table heaven has come upon us, and we confess that we are a people who walk in darkness. Thy love is upon us, and we are sore afraid. Thy mercy is upon us, and we are not worthy. Thy grace surrounds us, and we have little faith. As the bread is broken and the cup given in thy name, take from us our fear, make us worthy, renew our faith, and prepare us for the morning star descending to save us in our darkness, even Jesus Christ our Lord. Amen.

Now are we come again, dear Lord, to the time of the morning star, to thyself moving as azure into our darkness, as touch to our heaviness, as carol to our meagerness, as rose to our bitterness, as flesh to our emptiness. Thou art upon us as sky, hands, songs, garlands, tastes—making us thine in joy. Surely as we drink the red grape and eat the white bread, we shall be fed on mysteries, affectionate and deep, prepared for us before time was. Glory, glory, glory. Amen.

The Lord's Supper

January

Perhaps, God's greatest gift to man is that he has set each of us to live out our days confronted by our own mystery. That is to say, God has created human life with a variety and depth such as in our average way of living we scarcely dream of. We have a mystery and a glory within us, because we are the children of God. But most of the time we behave like orphans; because to accept our mystery means to accept God's mystery—and, therefore, to risk being in his presence often, which is not always a safe or pleasurable meeting. At the Lord's table we are invited to be exposed to the hidden depths within us as they are mirrored in the love and forgiveness of God. What we see, we will not always like to see; what we are given, we may desire to refuse. But if we hold fast, accept our mystery in God, we may yet find out who we really are.

The Lord's Supper — *January*

Almighty God, thou Mystery behind all things and flesh, thou who dost scatter stars and hold the daylight hours, thou Sky come down, thou endless One self-captured in our time, work in us thy miracle. Give us bread as heaven to keep our days tall and the cup as savior against the evil hour and death. Receive our prayers, and let our cries come unto thee; through Jesus Christ our Lord. Amen.

O God, we, who are so often caught between the slow jests of time and the quick and lovely solemnities of thy love, confess our sins, which are many; our loneliness, which is frequent; our emptiness, which comes hard. At this table, fashioned and fired by thy mystery, take us and build us into thy strength; burn away our dross and brighten us in true joy. O give us this day the daily bread of thy forgiveness; and let the cup of thine abiding mercies quench our thirst in the dry places; through Jesus Christ our Lord. Amen.

Almighty God, thy mercy is giant and thy love a vast circle around us. Fire breaks from thee, and grace abounds in the nights of our sorrow, in the dense dark of our pain. Thou art the solace of hands to our weariness and the true word of comfort to our loneliness. On the day of our defeat, thou canst trumpet us to storm the heights. A crust from thy bread, a syllable of thy word, a caress of thy love—and we are whole again, and the day splendors in laughter. Thou art Savior of all men, and holy is thy name. Amen.

The Lord's Supper

February

The Lord's Supper exposes us to an act of God by which he dramatizes for our sakes who he is and what he is like. He does so not verbally—that is, merely in words—but tangibly, so that in a way we can know him as a person rather than as an idea. God enacts in particular what he does for man's salvation. He shows us how man, everyman, possesses—whether he wants it or not—an eternal destiny and density. Man counts so much for God that God takes into himself man's suffering, despair, and very death. He does more in this feast. He gives us bread as he will give us bread in heaven. Indeed, in his name, this bread is already bread from heaven. He acts out in this meal how he redeems us.

Now at every point that we forget his act, we forget his mercy. But at every point we remember his act we receive his mercy—we participate in what his mercy means; namely, so ordering our lives that our lives are merciful and redemptive. We give back—or rather we act out—the mercy and the love which God has given us—a very tangible mercy.

The Lord's Supper February

O Lord, sovereign and holy, we have neither speech nor songs nor prayers nor understanding nor high thoughts nor heart's imagination to utter our thanksgiving; for heaven comes down to this table, and we taste bread for our rejoicing and drink the healing cup whereby we are made whole. O taste of the Lord for he is good and his mercy endures to all generations. Amen.

O God, whose name we cannot name, we live without you by our own choosing. We do not want you in our affairs seriously. We try to reduce you to our size and, therefore, lose you. Often, we feel shallow, empty, and defeated. We long for depth; we ache for fullness; we need satisfaction. Out of our little faith, we ask you to trouble us, find us, forgive us, and restore us. Let the bread and the wine of this plain meal be in us flesh and hope, lest we turn our backs on the mystery which lets us walk and run and enjoy. Amen.

Glory and honor to our God who prepares a table before us, who breaks bread that we may taste heaven, who pours wine that we may receive salvation. Blessing and honor to our God who feeds us himself that Love shall be incarnate in our blood, that Mercy shall wedge in our flesh, that Grace shall marrow in our bones. Blessing and honor and glory and power be unto Father, Son, and Holy Ghost forever and ever. Amen.

The Lord's Supper — *Ash Wednesday*

We live uneasily in a country and in a world that, for the most part, has chosen Caesar over God; and the chaos we have brought upon ourselves comes not from rendering unto Caesar that which is Caesar's but from rendering unto Caesar that which is God's: namely, the allegiance of our selfhood, our being, our souls. Like Esau, we have sold our birthright—to be the joyous sons and daughters of God—for a mess of pottage; that is, for the idolatry of things, power, social position, and make-believe. Alas, there are no words that can persuade men from a glittering emptiness that has the appearance of being full. Were Jesus himself to appear among us—offering in contemporary and lively language the choice of Caesar's coin and God's reconciling love—we would find most of the citizenry (including ourselves) too busy even to catch the irony of his offer. So we face a world where dissatisfactions with pious words, anger at hypocritical actions, give rise to incoherent shouts, distrust of other men's protestations of moral purity, and violence gathering to meet violence. When we cannot respond to the parable of Caesar's coin, we fall victim to Caesar.

The Lord's Supper

Ash Wednesday

Almighty God, thou who dost arise on the other side of all the stars and who in mercy cometh to the hearts of men, come now to our worship that what we do bears thy mark and thine eternity. Make us wrestle with thee. Cast us up against heaven. Wound us with the world's agony. Go into our days with us, so that what we are makes sense, so that what we hope has height. Capture us forever. Amen.

O God, there is in us transgression without name. There is the private hell. There is the purgatory of secret envy, adulterous wish, murderous thought, loveless ambition. There is the wilderness and the wild beasts and the devil. We do confess it all and cry thy mercy upon us to lead us out of the wasteland. Cleanse thou the evil in us that in the hidden places we may also worship thee with bright heart and the mind's pure devotion; through Jesus Christ our Lord. Amen.

O God, from the wilderness within us, we call upon thy name, and cry thy mercy, and beseech thee for a clear way and a light upon our way. We wander in forests, among beasts, torn by briars, beset by many fears. Open us a path from our sins, and return us to the house of the Lord, to thy plain table of bread and wine. Feed us upon forgiveness. Enliven us by grace. And restore us to the joy of thy salvation; through Jesus Christ our Lord. Amen.

The Lord's Supper — March

The Lord's Supper is always the table prepared in the presence of our enemies, provided that we understand that the word enemy must be extended to include the truth that a man is often his own best enemy. So we first receive this sacrament as it is given to us as we struggle with the dark and evil in ourselves. The first Lord's Supper—the Last Supper—was a gift of love in the midst of a betrayal, for example. Then, we can see that throughout history whenever and wherever the bread and drink were offered, it was always an event happening in the presence of man's sin. And so it is today. We are sinful people come to be nourished on that final divine love which alone can pardon us for what we do to one another. It is a meal of simplicity. It says that the way for men to eat together, to eat in peace in the presence of their evil, is to eat with God. God puts compassion in our hearts. He understands our evil. He gives thanks over bread being broken as life is broken; he forgives in the shadow of death. Even the outside enemies—the private or public foes—are embraced in his love. They are invited here with us.

The Lord's Supper — March

Lord who art Light beyond all light and Mercy underneath all mercies and Joy within all joys, we come by faith to thy table, desiring the bread of heaven for our faint and fearful souls and seeking the dark wine of salvation to put heart into our purpose and stride into our climb. Nourish us in depth and strengthen us in hope. Send us forth from thy feast to forgive as we have been forgiven; through Jesus Christ who is himself forgiveness. Amen.

O God, what shall be the measure of our sins but thine immeasurable mercies? Our wars blemish the earth. Our rich cities mock at the hungry. Our household lives run politely on without thee. O come we now to thy table penitent for ourselves and for the whole sick world, bringing our darkness for thy light and our misery for thy healing. Give us that bread which nourishes us bone and breath for mighty acts of love; and strengthen us with thy cup that runneth over; through Christ our Lord. Amen.

Receive, O Lord, our songs, our adorations, the drumbeats in us of our hope, the prayers hidden in our words, the sadness of our sin, the laughter in our flesh. For under the masks, our eyes seek thee. Under the lies, our minds want thee. Under the make-believe, our souls desire thee. Thy bread on our tongues gives joy. Thy drink in our bodies shapes us for salvation. Blessing and honor come in thy name. Amen.

The Lord's Supper — Maundy Thursday

When we participate in the Lord's Supper, we enter into God's darkness; that is, the nature of God that is unknown. If this feast did not arise in a mystery that defies our language, it would be no more than any other meal men share together. Its power would contain the frailty and limitation and blemish of mankind. The Lord's Supper, moreover, is in itself a metaphor of height and depth. It arises in mystery but stretches us to the very edges of that mystery. It casts us up against heaven and requires that we reach down into the very roots of our own being where we dare speak of the human soul. And yet despite its mystery and depth, we are invited to the table as men with our anxieties, our inconsistencies, our sin. Indeed, men like ourselves were the first guests at this table. Foolishness, pride, betrayal, lust, doubt—these and all the other sins and sicknesses of man were present as well as faith, trust, chastity, hope, love, and all the other virtues and joys of men. What makes the difference is that we break our bread and present our virtues and our sin before the living God.

The Lord's Supper — Maundy Thursday

O God, we come to thy mighty table with sin in us and around us. We carry a havoc in the blood which is against thee. We dwell among a people who forget thee. We burn but bear no light. We are indifferent and have no peace. Yet are we bound to thee as by a mystery, thou who art both Light and Peace. May the bread give us thy forgiveness and the cup refresh us with thy joy; through Jesus Christ our Lord. Amen.

How marvelous thy mercy, O Lord, that from our separate, casual, and crooked ways calls us to thy table, thy high feast of grace, thy plain meal of forgiveness. And here we are as Peter who denied thee thrice; as John and James priding to be first; as Matthew, publican and sinner; as Judas with his kiss of death; as everyman tangled in self-love, self-pity, and dark fear. O by the bread put flesh on the ribs of our thin souls, and from thy cup pour fire to kindle us to be thy people eager for joy and faithful in adoration. Amen.

For faith by which we take the plain fare of this meal, bread to put flesh on our souls and the drink of forgiveness to cool the fever of our sins; for hope that all men shall feast in the presence of the risen Lord; for love whereby the wheat and the grape within us nourish the small warmth into the large compassion; for health and promise and mercy lively within us: we praise God and glorify him and rejoice in him forever and ever. Amen.

Bread and wine are the elements of this holy feast we eat and drink. They are of the stuff of creation itself: the seed, the wheat field, and the vine. In them is symboled and actualized the work of man's hands—the planting, the tending, the harvesting, the mill, and the winepress. By them bodies live and around them men communicate and feed. Finally, bread and wine are the very flesh and blood of our Lord Jesus Christ, who is the Word made flesh. Yet there is even more; for the bread at this high and holy table is broken, the cup is given as a sacrifice, revealing that it is God's very nature to suffer for us—yea, even to die for us. The God who gives the seed to the sower and sets the vine upon earth that men may have food and drink for their bodies is also the God who offers his own body as bread and wine that men may have eternal food for their souls. And yet there is more. There is a Last Supper that omens Christ's death and sacrifice upon the cross, but there is also the first Lord's Supper when in an upper room the disciples eat the bread and drink the cup in the name of the risen Lord. This bread we break, this wine we drink, is ever and always to be received in the joy of Easter; for it is in truth food of the resurrection.

Thou who preparest a table before us, prepare us also who out of our poverty desire to come to thy feast. Move us by the miracle of thy presence among us to feel the mystery of thyself out of which all life is born and continues to be. Awaken us to both the sin and the goodness at warfare within us, making us sorrowful for the evil that we do and glad for the good that we can do. As, out of thy bounty, we may eat the bread of heaven, so may we help all men to eat the bread of earth. As, out of thy mercy, we may drink the cup of salvation, so may we care that every man be saved; through Jesus Christ who is the eternal Bread and the Promise of salvation. Amen.

O God, as we come this day to the Lord's table, prepare us inwardly to receive thy bread of forgiveness and thy cup of salvation. Help us by thy grace to be truly sorry for our sins, lest we come unworthily. Collapse our arrogance, disperse our vanities, destroy our lusts, that we may appear before thee out of our weakness and our need. And by thy mercy, feed us on those eternal joys by which sinners are forgiven, the sick are healed, and the dead are raised up, even the sacrifices and resurrection of our Lord Jesus Christ. Amen.

Great Lord, the bells and songs and tongues of all the earth shall praise thee. Morning itself arises and the night comes down to glorify thy name. And in the congregation thy people remember thy goodness to us and to all men. Especially we give thee thanks and endless adoration that this day we may sit at the heavenly banquet with the risen Lord, even Jesus Christ, unto whom with thee and the Holy Ghost, be all glory and majesty, dominion and power, world without end. Amen.

The Lord's Supper

The whole event of the Lord's Supper celebrates the difficult, the ambiguous, the necessary relationship between man and God. It is difficult, because to take the bread and cup is to identify with all that this feast recalls of suffering and requires of sacrifice. It is ambiguous, because we are never quite sure what does take place in the communion; or, to put it another way, man is not in charge of the miracle taking place. It is necessary, because, no matter how often we turn away from the depth and height of God, we again and again return for one more encounter; we have to find out if God is really there; we have to know if he is true.

Perhaps, most of all, this holy meal is a way of physically—even while symbolically—taking God into our hands and tangibly eating and drinking the stuff of heaven itself. But heaven is given in the things of earth. Grace comes to us in wheat and grape, in bread and wine, in death and resurrection.

The Lord's Supper May

Almighty God, from thy whirlwind come and speak to our hearts. Come with thy mercy, for we have need of it. Come with thy laughter, and teach us joy. Lay thy peace upon the world's rage; and unto all darkness, send thy light. Especially as we approach the celebrations of thy table, make us ready in body, mind, and soul to touch and taste and trust the holy mysteries before us. And send us forth, in thy strength, to heal and love and overcome. Amen.

O God, we come for bread, for the wheat of heaven, for the crust tasting of mercy. We come for drink, for the cup of love, for the refreshment which is salvation. Thou art this bread. Thou art this drink. Feed us thy sinew and thy strength. Brim over in us the waters and wines of thy forgiveness. For it is thyself shall mend our brokenness; it is thyself shall shake us from our sleep; it is thyself shall sing in us the songs of grace; through Jesus Christ our Lord. Amen.

Almighty God come down to manger size, fisherman's friend, parable-maker, swordsman against our lies, contender only for love, light for eyes and souls, donkey-rider, mercy's democrat against evil's kings, we praise thee for thyself among us; and we come to thy plain and holy table with thanksgiving. Thou art the broken Bread that makes us whole. Thou art the drinking Cup whereby we thirst no more. Glory to thy name forever. Amen.

The Lord's Supper

June

We should advance deeply in the aliveness of life itself if we were able so to participate in the Lord's Supper that we experienced almost tangibly how it reveals to us our essential nature, the truth of our humanness, the things that really matter. We hardly need to tell ourselves how we are worn and harried by a thousand things that do not matter, nor how much a day's business is playacting and exchanging one mask after another in the weary round of trying to find out who we really are. Thus, in both its simplicity and its vastness, the Lord's Supper offers us the refreshment of first things that, in the end, have always been first where men have matured and fulfilled themselves and possessed wholeness. It is a meal of universals, eternal facts of life that never pass away: the human miseries—poverty, sorrow, loneliness, fear, pain; and the human ecstasies—thanksgiving, joy, companionship, love, healing . . . taking place as all human acts take place—in the presence of God.

The Lord's Supper — June

Thou who hast led us to the golden season of the summer and brought us safely together to call upon thy name, to hear thy Word, and to offer up our intercessions for the sake of all mankind: be pleased to hear and accept our prayers, faltering and fragile though they be; and by the power of thy Holy Spirit turn our thoughts as one people to the deep places of thy mystery, which is the wellspring of the love which abides; and keep before us the love poured out in Jesus Christ, who brings us to this table to eat the bread of joy and drink the fire-filled wine. Amen.

O God, thy light arises over us, and we see our heavy dark. The bones in us weigh down with miseries, our minds are lazy, and our hearts grow dull. We have been meager in love and with love. We make boredom our companion and ornament our houses with indifference. We hear a terror stalking us even in the daylight. We run, we run, we run. Now at this table, turn us from our dark, our doldrums, and our death to take thy shining into us, to feed on thy mercies, and to come alive in thy grace. Amen.

Dear Lord, at this table the plain fare is thyself. Thy bread is angel, manger, hope, Samaritan. Thy cup is truth, cross, death, and alleluia. O burn on the tongues that dare to taste thee, and fire our flesh until it sings, and dazzle us until we turn to praise. Glory to God in the highest! Amen.

The Lord's Supper

July

If the small cup of mock wine and the crust of bread we take were our food for the day, a single day, we might be taught by this plain meal which we dare to call a holy feast. We would identify, for a little while, with the world's hunger. And yet the circumstance of our own affluence keeps this crumb and cup merely a symbol. We know of hunger but do not ever quite understand it; perhaps, because our own situation never seriously demands us to fast for more than a few hours. What we can be possessed by, in God's mercy, is a leanness of mind and soul: a mind unencumbered by the dishonesties and bias that have settled on our living, a soul persuaded that the vision of God is the single way to make lively and full of hope the vision of man. For this cup and bread are set forth and given us as the clear love of God in the midst of our betrayal. We are gathered to a meal that acts out the lean, unencumbered, pure compassion that God desires to put in the flesh and bone, heart, mind, and soul of every one of us.

The Lord's Supper

July

Almighty God, come upon us and overcome in us whatever keeps us from thee. Help us to desire thee in the occasion of all hours and to seek thee in the visible world we know best. Give us that faith that expects thy coming in every breath and the courage to declare thee before all men. Tell our hearts the way to the practice of mercy, and teach our souls to walk and run and hope to the lively measures of eternity. Continue us in every act that bears thy grace; through Jesus Christ our Lord. Amen.

Almighty God, who alone can sustain us among the snares and darkness everywhere around us, we have turned away from thy love; we have shunned thy wisdom; we have forgotten thy commandments. And in the times of suffering, in the places of injustice, we have too often hidden in our own pleasure and kept aloof from the fray. O somehow in thy mystery as we dare to eat thy bread and drink thy cup, return us to thyself and reestablish us in the community of man. Turn our good words to acts of compassion, and keep our lives true to the mercy revealed in Jesus Christ our Lord. Amen.

O gracious One, thou canst bid a star to be, turn home the summer robin, unravel the skeins of air, or wrap a world to sleep. Thou art might and heaven and the other side of dark. Thou art majesty. And yet thou dost set this table and bid us come and eat. O Majesty so meek! O Might so kind! O Heaven so near! Blessed art thou, O God. In thee shall be our joy forever and ever. Amen.

The Lord's Supper — August

There are times when the surrounding world carries a peace beyond us. The airs have a taste of heaven; the trees climb green and clean and lush. Our streets, our house, the to-and-fro traffic, all partake of an assurance that seems to arise in the very daylight or evening itself. We feel within us the presence of things transcendent. We walk and breathe within the world's "All's well." But what, of course, we also remember is that the nature that displays itself calmly in the summer days also presents itself with terror in the earthquake and the flood. The peace of the most serene horizon never quite answers the deepest human needs for peace and meaning. It is in response to these deepest needs arising in the very marrow of man that we participate in the peace and meaning of the Lord's Supper. Here is an action, tangible, intimate, human, that declares for peace in the very presence of the earthquake and flood. Here meaning abides within and beyond disaster. Here is the true transcendence.

The Lord's Supper — August

O thou who art before all beginnings and after all endings and yet art miracle among us every day, we pray thee to keep our now in thy foreverness and to mark us hand and bone, heart and mind, with thine eternal mercies. Among the fats and frostings and the cream, keep us lean and hungry for heaven's bread. And cause us to be athirst for the deep drink of thy forgiveness and hope whereby the lame walk and the blind see and the prisoners are set free; through Jesus Christ our Lord. Amen.

Hear, O Lord, the confession of our hearts and cleanse us thoroughly of our sins that by faith we may dare to come to thy table. Surely we have fled from thy love, watered down thy truth, and held many other gods before thee. We muddle against the disciplines that would give us life and smirk and chirrup at the holy gifts that would give us joy. O so feast us this day on the bread that does not perish that we may arise to new daylights of hope, and give into our hands the cup of forgiveness which makes us whole again; through Jesus Christ our Lord. Amen.

We praise thee, our God, for days that spin and shower with to-and-fro-borne birds; for children at baseball; for true pity binding up wounds; for the dialogues of love and hands that tell stories; for the times of mourning and the places of hope; for despair's defeat in the days of trust; and for the endless comfort of sleep in the huge nights. We come rejoicing to thy table. Let the bread speak! Let the cup sing!—to thy glory and for our peace; through Jesus Christ our Lord. Amen.

The Lord's Supper — September

All has not been well in the Christian church. We who are the inheritors of the roaring lion which was the Reformation have, for the most part, brought forth a mouse. Or, to put it another way, while we have added a few decorative bricks to the temple and blown a few sophisticated flourishes on our trumpets so that the world will know that we are still in business, we have not heeded the Gospel's warning: "What doth it profit a man (or the church) if he gain the whole world and yet loses his soul, his life?" We are simply not clear in our hearts and minds as to why the church exists, and we participate in its life on levels of unreality that would never satisfy us in our households or on our job. We pantomime even at the Lord's Supper.

Yet here where the bread is broken and the cup given the true life of the church is visibly enacted. Here we are thrust up against the mysteries of life and death. Here we encounter the sovereign purpose of the church—to be the broken body that the world may be whole. Here we enter the regions of man's joy because God is in this with us affirming the paradox that the church that loses its life will gain it.

The Lord's Supper — September

Almighty God, whose hands hold the hurricane and the sun's fire and the houses of the night and to whom the walks of space are a very little thing, come to this feast wherein we dare to touch thy lightning and handle thy glory. Let us chew the eternal bread and drink the dews and dawns of life that existed before man was. And send us out to take into our bodies the broken body of the world; through Jesus Christ our Lord. Amen.

We come to thy table, Lord, confessing, each of us, his own sin: the private evil thou alone can hear, the indwelling sickness thou alone can heal, the hidden prides of heart and mind and soul which thou alone can see. And we confess together our sin as a church, and beseech thy mercy for our make-believe, our flirtation, and our escape. O in the breaking of the bread, give our shadow a substance; and cause us to drink deep the fathomless cup that we may thirst no more. Amen.

For this hour, this now, this instant racing to its end yet brimming with thine endlessness, we praise thee, O eternal God. For this self, body, flesh, bone, breath, forever falling yet forever held, we praise thee, O redeeming Lord. For this life, this fragment, this patch, this brokenness that finally in thyself is mended, we praise thee, O thou healing Lord. For this earth dark but always in thy light, for this bleak loneliness that cannot be alone because of thee, for this day's fear that thou dost overbrim with love, we praise thee, O thou shining God. Thou givest us thyself and thereby gladness. Blessed is thy name forever. Amen.

A man matures when he confronts his darkness, when he lets the depth of his experience shake and uproot the hothouse blossoms cluttering the topsoil of his life. We are moved by dark tides of desire and dream, rich streams of memory and longing, rivers of anguish and loneliness, deep pools of joy that are lost within us; and underneath the surfaces of our normal living are subterranean flows of the hidden and mysterious by which so much of life is driven and fulfilled. This darkness, this depth are, in a sense, the pillar of cloud and fire that lie between us and life, between us and God. And the only way is through the darkness, not around it, nor running in another direction. This darkness is not subject to our laws, our explanations, or our moral codes.

It is the darkness that everywhere breaks through the Lord's Supper; it is the depth of the bread grown in the earth and the body broken that is returned to the earth. It is the grape from rooted vines in fertile soil and the blood shed in the mysterious rite of sacrificial dying. It is the depth in which joy seeds itself and the darkness in which grace shines.

The Lord's Supper

O God, thou Dark, thou Depth, thou Dawn, come to us as mystery, come to us as height, come to us as sun, so that we may know awe and hope and rejoicing. Make us unsure in our own conceits. Trouble us with heaven. Strike our matchsticks with thy lightning. And at thy holy feast feed us thyself. Give us thy Bread so that we will not perish. Give us thy Drink whereby we thirst no more. And send us forth to sing thee in the world, to live thy mercies, and to bear thy love; through Jesus Christ our Lord. Amen.

O God, our Comforter, there is no ease in confessing our sins. What we say together of the evil in us all cries out for pardon. And yet there is more. We do confess, each of us, his private sins, the sins hidden, the sins we wrestle with alone in the dark places. O by the mystery of thy largest love, let the bread which is life and the wine which is forgiveness replenish us, that we may have a solace in thee, that we may have a holiness and a felt mercy to stay us in our time of need; through Jesus Christ our Lord. Amen.

O thou great God who, with thanksgiving, broke bread for our hunger and gave us drink for our thirst, continue in thy mercy to feed us always on thyself. And so be in our kitchen life, the labor of our hands, the hope of our hearts, the shape of our souls, that we shall hereafter always desire the bread and grail of thy salvation. O prepare us mightily for thy meat and fire set before us this day. Amen.

The Lord's Supper — November

There is an iron edge to life, a minor key sung and sighing through all choruses we sing; there are the tides of anger, the motions of hate, the falling of boredom—all these hardnesses over and against us. And we must admit to them and turn and face them and go through them. For they exist. They are part of the truth. Indeed, they are solemnly present in the celebration of the Lord's Supper. They are betrayal, flight, and crucifixion. They are the sin of man and the terror of all the ambiguous evil of the world.

Yet here we also celebrate eucharist and thanksgiving, the world of the resurrection and the hand of God strong against the deaths we die and compassionate toward the sins we commit. It is the joy of God infiltrating into all the emptiness of the daily round and making lively and full of grace the very routines that without grace we find so deadly. It is everything in our experience that we remember and lay hold upon which causes us to shout with the psalmist: "This is the day that the Lord hath made. We will be glad and rejoice in it."

O thou who givest thyself in this plain feast that we may be redeemed by forgiveness and refreshed by love, be with us always in the breaking of the bread. Help us to see thee shining out and gathered to a greatness in all visible things; and let thy grace be lively upon us and in us where the hands work, the mind wonders, and the soul dreams. And when our eyes are blurred and our hearts are fearful, hold us yet more tenderly in the mercy of thy means, until out of our deepest needs we turn again to thee. Amen.

O God, no matter what the blithe exterior, our lives are piecemeal, poor, and plundered by our sin; for our sin hath a torment, making us fearful within and evil toward the neighbor and the stranger. Except for thee, we are shadows and dead leaves. O ingather us to thy table and feed us on the solid bread of love and quicken us with Christ's cup of joy. For we would rise this day to be whole men and people of thy praise; in Jesus' name. Amen.

Surely we were nothings, zeros, emptiness, until you breathed upon us and the pulses sang. You are our God and holy is your name. Surely we wake because you have kept the watch; we walk and run in the strength of your Bread; we drink joy only from your Cup. You are our God and holy is your name. Surely you are sword against evil, comforter against loss, shield against terror, defender against sin. You are our God and holy is your name. Amen.

The Lord's Supper

The bread and wine of the Lord's Supper are things of simplicity that lead us into wonder and depth. It is not hard to understand bread and wine in themselves. It makes sense to eat and drink. In fact, so much in the Gospels: the figures about the kingdom of God, the parables, the words of Jesus in the Sermon on the Mount, Jesus' birth, death, and resurrection—all arise out of well-known human experience, simple events opening onto the vast. Yet we are daily—all of us—caught up in the complicated, tiring busyness of keeping going in the twentieth-century world. More and more, we become entangled in a clutter of nonessentials to which we devote most of our time, energy, and substance. This is the day of the experts who know more and more about less and less. Life is mostly on the surface, and what a web of circumstance we are dangled in. Somewhere, somehow, we remember that men were intended to live joyously and deeply together; we live hostilely and emptily apart, even though we are clustered together like ants. The hero, indeed, the saint of our time would be that man—or those men—who could show us the way out of nonessentials that are forever choking out our living.

The Lord's Supper

We praise thee, most gracious Lord, for thyself among us in the daily round, beside us in the days of our tribulation, behind us in the times of our remembering, and before us in our seasons of rejoicing. We praise thee for this table before us, for thyself as host, for the mysterious bread and cup that feed us thy holy love and quicken our lives with salvation. Blessed art thou, O sovereign and redeeming Lord. Amen.

O God come down from heaven to give us heaven's bread, we are not worthy of this feast. We are sinners who do not hope enough, who do not love enough, who do not trust enough. We are ashamed, and we dare to come to thy table not because we are good but in the name of Jesus Christ who came not to cast out sinners but to save them. Amen and amen.

Let us rejoice among the motorcars and spaceships; let us sing in the presence of the darkness of war; let us exult among flower gardens and comfortable houses; let us shout for joy as the world comes tumbling down—that God at this table gives us all that we need eternally—food and forgiveness and himself. Praise him who is our health and salvation. Amen.

The Lord's Supper

Perhaps, we should find another phrase for "the kingdom of God"—we who have overthrown kings. Could we say "the country of the soul"—that life we live when we are totally alive, when the work, the day, people come upon us and find us lively and responsive with a center of meaning, a depth of being which is able to give each thing, and event, and person a true value? This center, this depth, this country will have its first allegiance, its significant awareness, in the God whose ways are higher than our ways. Or, to put it another way, we will be citizens of the country of God. This, indeed, may be what it means to have a soul, a being, a life. "Blessed is he," cries a man in Jesus' presence, "who eats bread in the kingdom of God, in the country of the soul!" Blessed is that man whose daily life feeds on depth, who celebrates his life in God. Surely, the taking of the bread and wine at the Lord's table urges us into the country of the soul, the city of God, . . . that way of handling life that makes of the most ordinary moment and place a part of the timeless landscape which is given of God.

The Lord's Supper

Glory to God! He fashions the worlds and they are in his keeping. He furnishes the earth with good things and sends the circling winds and hurries the rains. His air is for our breath and his light prepares its coming for our rejoicing. Glory to God! It is he who stands beside us in the night vigil. It is he beside us carrying our griefs. He gives us Bread for life and a Cup wherein to drink our resurrection. Glory to God. Amen.

Majestic One, we come to thy table not ready and not worthy. We are a little too fat for heavenly food. We have no awe any more for the holy places. Yet we have come for some bread and some drink that will save us. Our wild beasts are with us—the lion greed, the jackal fear, and the elephant indifference. Tame them and us, O Lord, and kneel us down that we may receive this mystery out of our deepest need and with thanksgiving; through Jesus Christ our Lord. Amen.

Thou art before all things, unbegun, yet beginning everything. Thou art after all things, at time's end, yet unending. Thou art beyond everything that was and is and shall be. Among men, thou art as water to thirst, as fire to cold, as life to death. Thy crust of poverty makes all men rich. Thy chalice is the drink of endless grace. Praise be to thee forever. Amen.

Seasons

Winter

Praise the Lord from the earth,
    ye dragons, and all deeps:
Fire, and hail; snow, and vapors;
    stormy wind fulfilling his word:
Mountains, and all hills;
    fruitful trees, and all cedars . . .

from Psalm 148

Canticles Winter

Now cold days come
And the singing of birds has gone.

Grass dries, air spins white with winds.
Eyes look through trees and beyond.

Men march to fear and loneliness.
We are not wise in our own conceits.

But you turn us to taste the given world,
To live within each other's love.

You made us for joy even in the bleak season.
Praise to your name, you whom we cannot name. Amen.

Lord, the morning has come.
The voice of thy mercy is heard in our fields.
The gray birds of winter sing of the airs of forgiveness.

The leafless tree and the sere grass are faithful.
The wind is the sharp taste of joy.
All proclaim thee. All praise thee!

Blessed be thou, O Majestic!
Thou art our Strength and our Redeemer
In every season and even forever. Amen.

For the day's eye open upon us;
For the tall air that comrades beside us
And is a lover within us;
For snow mountained and meadowed,
And children with skates and red-mittened;
For boys all drum and guitar, and girls dancing;
For men who laugh at themselves,
And women gentle as bells;
And for grace, dazzle, smile, wink, skip, wave,
hello, handshake,
We praise our God who comes, is here, is now. Amen.

Canticles Winter

Great is the Lord and greatly to be praised!

All things are his: the wintertime,
The ring and wrack and the cold,
The wind's run cross-country and white,
Skies wild, skies merciful and blue,
And everyday the light among us,
Light leaping toward the spring.

And we are his: our silences
Hear him making and gathering,
Giving and withholding,
Exclaiming and listening.
Bones wake and walk and run.
Eyes look, hearts love, souls dream.

Great is the Lord and greatly to be praised.
Amen.

O God, your gifts abound where we are:
The dart and whirl of winter birds,
Snowfall on hills and drift in the valleys,
Children booting home from school,
Food and laughter at the table,
Hands that sew and bake,
Love walking toward us.

So much, so much, and everywhere
And everyday given over and over!
And yourself, in the midst of it all:
Calling our names,
Clearing the way,
And keeping the watch!
Amen and amen and amen.

Canticles Winter

Praise God
That children shall have their holiday in snow,
That boys and girls shall love and marry,
That birds fly blue and gray and white by our windows.

Praise God
That we know what it is to be lonely,
That weeping and rejoicing go on in the same cities,
That suffering wounds us all.

Praise God
That this season is ours but also his,
That the dying are in his keeping,
That every man arises to a new day.

Praise Father, Son, and Holy Ghost. Amen.

Lord of the universe
And all that is therein: the spaces of the dark,
The pulses of the stars, the cool light and the fires!

Lord of this earth:
The green seas ranging and the small ponds,
The mountains in snow and the hills in soft haze,
Quick winds and gentle and black storms,
Rock fields and the prairie's ocean,
Village in white and city in stone!

Lord of all men:
Breath for our birth, song for our life,
Trumpet for our death! time's alleluia!

Praise to you now and forever! Amen.

Canticles Winter

Yea God, we are glad in thee, and sing thee,
And declare thee, who art joy to the mourners,
A new music to them that be bowed down,
The Word of hope for the lost.

Thou art as daylight to our murk and dark.
Thou art as burning against our cold.
Thou art the sky blue above our winter
And the stirring in the dead ground.

O that our tongues had the burning
And our eyes the daylight and our hands the sky
And our hearts the stirring that we might praise thee!

Thy gifts are always given. They are now!
And thy glory is always breaking around us. Amen.

Dear Lord, our hearts are unfeignedly thankful
For the day's eye, the sun,
And the great azure, the sky;
For trees, the catchers of the winds,
And hills, the snow-bearers;
For all things hastening, waiting,
Hoping toward the spring.

We praise you for what is given, what we did not earn:
The song, the child, the dream, the love, the day!

We praise you
For our hands when they heal,
Our bones when they hope,
Our hearts when they show mercy,
Our minds when they speak truth.

You made us for delight.
Blessed is thy name forever. Amen.

Spring

For, lo, the winter is past,
the rain is over and gone;
The flowers appear on the earth;
the time of the singing of birds is come,
and the voice of the turtle is heard in our land.

from the song of Solomon

Canticles Spring

Lord, the clouds of thy spring arrive.
The air breathes new days.
Cold and dark and the winter death go from us.

And within us the dance begins,
And the high songs run,
And thy laughter bears promises.

Thy season is forever glad
And thy weather is anthem.

O be within us always
That in thee we stand in joy
Against storm and all evil.

Praise be to Father, Son, and Holy Ghost. Amen.

O Lord, the soft rains run, earth thaws,
And the sun follows the robins on the lawn.
Holy and blessed is thy name!

Children singsong, farmers wave, puddles shine.
Holy and blessed is thy name!

I love, you love, he loves, we love, they love!
Holy and blessed is thy name! Amen.

Almighty God, the season proclaims thee.
Thy grace and gladness everywhere abound.

All things and creatures praise thee.
Praise! cry the fields and the brookstreams.

Praise! sing the orchard robins.
And Praise! sigh the mourning doves.

Praise! says the south wind.
Praise! shout the hills.

Let everything that hath breath
Praise the Lord! Amen.

Canticles Spring

Now come the jonquil days
And the airs for new hearts.
Winds look white
And branches toss
And hope is
In the up and down.

Everywhere, O everywhere,
Are grackle, cowbird,
Redwing, robin,
Blue jay, finches,
Purple, gold;
And morning waking
To the mourning doves.

O God, you come to us
In colors, skies,
The days, the nights,
In touch, dream, smile.
O marvelous, fabulous, great
Is your coming among us. Amen.

Now God sends forth the springtime.
All things are new.
He covers the earth with the south winds
And soaks the fields with warm rains.

He opens the air with sunlight,
And the leaves shelter the trees.
Our hearts are made glad,
And he leads us into the work with rejoicing.

The dark winter tales,
The stories of sadness are over.
He walks on our land
Shouting his word of redemption.

He calls us to follow,
To praise, forever and ever. Amen.

Canticles Spring

Now is the time of bluebirds on wires,
The flowering earth,
The taste of the easy rain,
The coming on of the green and holy twilights.

God's hand is in this.
He who gives storms, gives calm.
Praise to his name, his power, his peace.

And where the heart loves and the mind wonders,
In the miracle of breath and in the march of bone—
Moves in upon us, gathering and keeping,
The Holy Ghost, the Comforter.

And in Christ's strength—hands heal,
The broken mend, the lame dance, the dead arise.
Glory, then, to Father, Son, and Holy Ghost. Amen.

We praise the Lord. We live because he is.
He sends this day, he and no other.

We wake in the morning, and he goes before us.
We count our children, and they are his gifts.

This spring is his, all in leaf green,
The choirs from treetops, and the easy rain.

He makes the noon drowse, sets the ancient sun,
And lets the downfall of the evening come again.

In his hands also are our sins, our death,
Which he has overcome for all our sakes!

Praise, then, the Lord, all ye his people,
And be glad! Amen. Amen. Amen.

You send airs belled with song,
And soft colors
Ripple and comb on lawn and field.

You come also to the human heart,
Giving us joy and rainbows of hope,
Whether the times be dry or dying or cold.

You are our Savior. You indwelling in us,
We become seasons, burgeoning, blossoming,
Lively, and all love. Holy is your name. Amen.

O God, we turn to see the ancient sky,
Its canopy of blue over and upon us.

Airs run in soft yellows, reds;
In snowfall orchards we behold your glory.

Yea, against the evil weather within
You set the brimming days!

And you call us to remember, when we fail and fall,
These times of grace, these leaping hours.

O on our tongues the heart's thanksgivings rise!
Amen.

Praise him, the sovereign Lord,
The Fashioner of light, the Urger of seasons.
He sends the blessed spring
And bright and whispering beginnings.

Praise him, the lofty Ariser,
Who says to the darkness: Be morning!
Who exclaims to our fears: Be love!
Who cries to our lostness: Be found!

Praise him, the holy Invader.
He redeems us from vanity and death,
From body's angers and soul's loneliness.
Praise Father, Son, and Holy Ghost! Amen.

Canticles Spring

For thyself among us daily and always
As strength for the work,
As joy for the hours,
As bulwark against all evil:
We give thee thanks.

For this good earth havening the seasons,
Springtimed now in white,
Lively in soft winds,
And finally blessed by being held in thee:
We give thee thanks.

For men who go with love
And women who walk in grace
And children who dance all new
And saints who are laughter:
We give thee thanks.

Thy bounty is ever upon us! Amen.

O God, you give us the Maytime:
The snow orchards and the red quince,
Airs tantalizing, and the running grass.
Everywhere, over and under, your love abounds,
And we live in your gladness.

O let the taste of your joy
Be on our tongues as praise;
And let the bells of your mercy
Be robin and hope in our ears.
The world dances in you.
Amen.

Canticles Spring

O God from whose bounty comes
All blessedness to man's heart:

The green wash of the air,
Whistlings that awake in trees;

Love in the orchard walks,
Hope in the blossomings;

Handclasps of courage
And drums in the soul—

You made all things
And set man in your landscape.

You are the sufferer
Who knows our wounds.

You are the comforter
Who heals our diseases.

Blessed is your name forever. Amen.

Our hearts have a music, O Lord:
The talk of the small brooks,
The wake-up and sigh of the mourning doves,
The wind-fall snow in the orchards,
Shout for the home run on the common,
Hurrah for the green and turning world!

Thou art the music, O Lord,
Who giveth each thing in its season.
Thou art the song eternally new.
Sing in us gladly forever. Amen.

Summer

Thou visitest the earth and waterest it;
Thou makest it soft with showers;
Thou crownest the year with thy goodness,
    and thy paths drop fatness.
They drop upon the pastures of the wilderness,
    and the little hills rejoice on every side.
The pastures are clothed with flocks;
    the valleys also are covered with corn;
    they shout for joy; they also sing.

from Psalm 65 (adapted)

Canticles Summer

See how God comes to us
In great blocks of light and dark,
In the first mornings, in day-drawn seasons,
In Junes of ripening, in the side-yard rose.

See how God's Son shapes in his body
The Father's love for us
And his judgment upon us.

See, as a fine sifting wind,
God's Spirit blowing a mystery
Up, under, and around
The dollar bills, the prestige, and the power—
Saying, "Be born again, be new, be loved." Amen.

As air is bright,
And orioles arouse the elms,
And taste is lilac rare,
And meadows run:
We praise thy world and thee, O Lord.

As boys swing bats,
And neighbors mow and wave,
And farmers scythe and bale,
And girls adorn:
We praise thy world and thee, O Lord.

As just men act,
And all men are samaritan,
And towns are open towns,
And every man has worth:
We praise thy world and thee, O Lord.
Amen.

Canticles Summer

Now moves upon us God's summertime, the long daylight,
The drowse and the hum, and the distant quiet.

Now are birdsongs in thickets,
And hills in haze, and backyards in shade.

Now are secret ripenings in fields,
And boys growing tall,
And the green evening around our houses.

God in his pleasure gives us this season.
The airs declare him and his glory.
He surrounds us with his love.

Praise him for summer and the changing year
And the years of our lives.

Praise him for the outward signs
And the inward grace.

Praise him for Jesus Christ and the dazzling resurrection
And for the Holy Ghost whose peace is over all. Amen.

The days of the week have stood
Blue and spacious, holy and tall,
And God is in the midst of them.
Praise ye the Lord.

Our houses abide. There is food on the table.
Children still somersault,
And our days brim with the brooks of their laughter.
Neighbor trusts neighbor,
And God is in the midst of them.
Praise ye the Lord.

Terror may come, and the earth shake,
And man's folly lay waste the brittle cities.
Death is an old comrade.
But God is in the midst of all the world,
And all men shall live in his mercy forever.
Praise ye the Lord.
Amen.

Canticles Summer

O Lord, your summer is come,
And everywhere field grasses rise.
Your trees are thick green,
Your days are canopied in sun and blue,
And there are squares of shade.

Around us the warm sounds.
Above us the high sounds.
Beside us such speech and hum
As sets the heart dancing.

So you give shiningly;
And the soft rains come,
And the land blossoms and sings;
So your largess comes to us.

Let our lives praise you
In our houses, on the streets;
And with our hands open
Let us enact your mercy among all men.

Through Jesus Christ our Lord. Amen.

Yea, Lord, we give thee thanks
For this day and all our yesterdays;
For good days and bad days,
For days of hope and days of despair,
For days of losing and days of finding.

And we praise thee especially
For the lofty open pause of summer:
A pasture running to a hill,
A pool and a deer,
Many birds in the mornings
And their soft talk in the evenings,
And sleep drifting in
After the games and the run and the people.

Under it, over it all, most gracious Lord,
We hear and touch thyself.
Amen.

Canticles Summer

Glory be to God
For daytimes, hay tastes,
Sun-sprawl, noon-high sounds;
For singsong boys and hopscotch girls;
For quick birds, hedge-chirps,
Elm tree afternoons;
For meadow upon meadow,
Haze and green,
And evening coming down,
And dark and sleep.
He fathers forth whose beauty is past praise!
Praise him. Amen.

O Majesty, O Magnificence, O Mystery, come!
Be hammer, and break our indifference.
Be sun, and splinter our shadows.
Be wind, and scatter our despair.

Yea, in the dry country of our souls,
Let thy grace rain;
So that we take root in thee, and grow.

Make of us trees strong in all seasons,
Bearing good fruit,
Giving shade to all weariness
And shelter to them that are lost.

So we pray to the glory of Jesus Christ
Who made the crosstree
Green and flourishing forever.
Amen.

Canticles Summer

All summer the days come to us, various, wide,
From mornings of meadows
Into the green dark and the nightfall of stars.

We heard the weather gathering, coming and going;
Small birds were among the berries;
The grasses dried,
And we felt our hearts in their swaying.

And, then, always the trees,
The great combs of shade in our yards,
And the hundred thousand leaves for our watching.

All was good and gift and grand!
And the days come on; the gift is still given.
Thy goodness stays. Thy grandeur stands. Amen.

Praise be to God
For his surrounding world,
The field's drowse and the sky's silence,
Blue weeds at roadsides and pheasants running,
Green evenings, and night come down with fireflies.

Praise be to God
For handshakes and galloping children,
Words of love and rollicking laughter.

Praise be to God
For healing in the midst of hate,
Sight in the times of blindness,
Freedom in the places of slavery,
And hope in the ages of despair.

Praise be to God. Amen.

Canticles Summer

Now autumn waits,
And still the summer air is green.
God stands by the morning.

Cool tastes in the winds
And burn touches the trees.
O cities of men awake!
And villages ring out!

Speak of his beauty in the noondays,
And when the afternoons turn warm and yellow,
Tell of him tenderly.

Our God is in the season.
Even now, he wanders the inner country,
Where the heart hills and the soul mountains.
Sing of him boldly! Amen.

Lord, for the cañadas of air
Come down upon us cold and blue;

For goldenrod roadsides
And waxwings on wires;

For the schoolboy trudging
And gaming to himself;

For an orchard walk
And the clustered sumac;

For this world now and the taste of it,
The sound of it, the sight of it;

For the touch of rough
And odors tantalizing;

For what you give to us within
As we wake, work, hope, sleep, dream:

We praise you a shouting and forever praise!
Amen.

Autumn

For the Lord thy God bringeth thee into a good
land, a land of brooks of water, of fountains
and depths that spring out of valleys and hills;
a land of wheat and barley, and vines, and fig
trees, and pomegranates; a land of olive oil and
honey; a land wherein thou shalt eat bread without
scarceness, thou shalt not lack anything in it.

from Deuteronomy 8 (adapted)

Canticles Autumn

Lord, it is time!
Your touch burnishes the fields.
Roadsides are aster, goldenrod, and dry.
Man turns to the work
And sees fire break from the trees.

Lord, it is time!
You give another season—
The days of apple and brimming and arriving.
Man turns to the work
And hears hope on the crisp air.

Lord, it is time!
You send eternity in the hours—
The colors of celebration.
Man turns to the work
And touches his own resurrection.

Lord, it is time!
Amen.

Now is the season emblazoned and fire-full.
Airs run clean.
Our houses stand by thy mercy.
The speech of light ripples our fields
And speaks thy glee-song to us.

Yea, Lord, thou art the morning of our rising;
Thou art the noonday that neighbors us with love;
And in the evenings thou wilt go with us into the long sleep,
Keeping the night watch until the new day comes.
Praise be to thee, our God, forever and ever. Amen.

Canticles Autumn

O God, everywhere the gold has shaken down;
And the walks are wanders and wonders
Of russet, of blaze, and of green.

You give fields
And the tawny grass catching the winds.
You tangle cold in the orchards
And crisp the pumpkin heaps.

Surely your harvest is in our hearts;
And your joy is in us
Tumbled high, pressed down, and running over.

Blessed are your hands upon us this day
And blessed are all seasons. Amen.

Ah, God, be praised, be praised,
For thou art here!
This drift-gold season is thine;
The chill and apple-red on air,
The football voices and the early dark,
All are in thee!

We are in thee.
We wake, we walk in thee!
And down the new daylights,
And into the miles of night ahead,
It is thyself keeps the watch against peril;
It is thyself bears the clamorous joy!

Ah, God, be praised, be praised!
Amen.

Canticles Autumn

Lord,
Thy season runs tawny in the fields.

Feathers and blaze are thy hills,
And all airs are golden.

Sun and blue and apple and cold
Are thy colors; wind is thy taste.

Thy touch is dry leaves,
And the breath of the grape teaches us.

We hear thee at night marching the geese,
And thy peace is under the dark of stars.

O blessed Giver, always the world is thine.
Amen.

This day, this day crisps
As the mists hover the meadows.
Grasses dry and bronze;
Weeds climb in colors.

Hear the wind bring
The blue north to our doorsteps.
Taste the apple airs.
Touch the elm gold.

Everywhere the fire dance begins
And the hidden drummers beat in our blood.

Oh, the Maker of heaven and earth is in this.
He gives these days we do not earn.

He maketh in us a joyful noise.
He sings us into the high season.

Glory glory glory. Amen.

Canticles Autumn

O God, we praise thee for the eyes' look:
Tree fire, asters at roadsides, pageant hills.

We praise thee for the tongue's taste:
Odors of smoke and haze and apple and sun.

We praise thee for the ear's listening and the hand's touch:
Geese going down the night, round golds and shapes of harvest.

We praise thee for the heart's love,
And the mind's radar, and the soul's expectations.

We praise thee for these and all thy gracious mercies;
Through Jesus Christ, our sovereign and saving Lord.
Amen.

Lord, such daylights are upon us:
The running gold,
The reds casting spells,
The burnish abroad on the fields,
The mists sifting.

And such noondays under the dazzle:
Asters at roadsides,
Orchards tumbling their apples,
The wide sky,
And the cock pheasant's whirring.

And such evenings coming:
With the dark and tang,
Dew bearding the green lawns,
The autumn stars flying overhead,
And the good sleep arriving.

Lord, such days!
And now this gift of bread
For walking true,
And this cup of life
To send us forth singing!
Amen.

Canticles Autumn

Lord, all is ready.
Our hearts wait.
Earth brims to its dying.

Sun is in the trees,
And burn is in the fields,
And hillsides go deeper than scarlet.

Leaf meal is under our walks.
The season is ripening
And fading and going.

Thou art everywhere:
In the full fire and after the full fire,
In the flame's going and in the embers.

All is ready.
We see thee in the dying, the death, and beyond.
Glory be to Father, Son, and Holy Ghost.
Amen.

Now, Lord, at the turning season,
The air dries, and the dark comes soon.

Now are the trees windows,
And the eyes see distances.

You are in the sere mornings and the falling night.
You are where the dying is and the going away.

In you we hear new winds driving despair with hope
And clearing every weariness with joy.

In you we look beyond,
And praise, praise, praise. Amen.